ALL-TERRAIN
PUSHCHAIR WALKS
The North York Moors

Rebecca Terry & Zoë Sayer

Published by Sigma Leisure – an imprint of
Sigma Press, 5 Alton Road, Wilmslow, Cheshire SK9 5DY, England.

British Library Cataloguing in Publication Data
A CIP record for this book is available from the British Library.

ISBN: 978-1-85058-842-9 (13-digit); 1-85058-842-2 (10-digit)

Typesetting and Design by: Sigma Press, Wilmslow, Cheshire.

Cover Photograph: The Bridestones *(Copyright, Phillip Elsdon).*

Maps and graphics: Rebecca Terry and Zoë Sayer

Photographs: Rebecca Terry, Zoë Sayer, Keith Jackson, Tracy Whale and Phillip Elsdon

Printed in Poland – Polskabook UK

Disclaimer: the information in this book is given in good faith and is believed to be correct at the time of publication. No responsibility is accepted by either the author or publisher for errors or omissions, or for any loss or injury howsoever caused. Only you can judge your own fitness, competence and experience. Do not rely solely on sketch maps for navigation; we strongly recommend the use of appropriate Ordnance Survey (or equivalent) maps.

Preface

The North York Moors national park encompasses varied and beautiful scenery within the eastern reaches of North Yorkshire. This book contains thirty tried and tested pushchair walks distributed throughout the park showing you the best it has to offer. The routes include riverside walks, rambles through the heather moors and coastal strolls. There are abbeys, castles, railways and country estates to see on route as well as natural features such as valleys filled with wild daffodils and holes created by giants! The area has so much to see and is surrounded by legend making it the perfect place to introduce your children to the delights of the outdoors. An early introduction to walking will give them a healthy outlook for the future and a great understanding of their environment.

All terrain pushchairs have brought the great outdoors to our doorsteps. There is no longer any reason why having a baby should deter us from getting out and about. The North York Moors is a fantastic area in which to use these pushchairs as it has an extensive network of paths and bridleways. However, it is impossible to plan a walk from a map as details of terrain and obstacles such as stiles and narrow kissing gates are not available. We have selected thirty pushchair-friendly walks which will allow you to go for a walk with full knowledge of the route ahead.

The thirty walks contained within this book were selected to demonstrate the diversity of scenery in this beautiful national park. There are a variety of walk grades from simple strolls around lakes and reservoirs to more ambitious moorland and coastal rambles. Many of the walks have shortening options and get out of trouble clauses! Walk selection is simple with our 'at a glance' key with the added advantage of extra information on refreshments etc. Every walk has background information about the area and a selection of 'in the area' activities for other ways to amuse yourselves and the kids while you are there.

We have really enjoyed putting this book together and hope that you and your children enjoy the walks as much as we did.

Rebecca Terry & Zoë Sayer

Acknowledgements

Thanks to Jamie, Sam, Rhodri and Rhiannon for making these walks so much fun and to Phil and Keef for all their help. Thanks also to Chris, Tracy and Alex and to Jamie and Sam's grandparents, Nan and Peter Terry and Maggie and Roger King, who joined us for many of the walks.

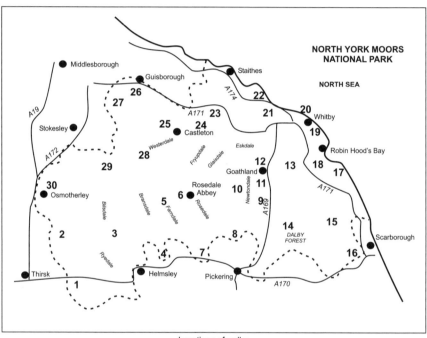

Locations of walks

Contents

Introduction

This book contains thirty walks in the North York Moors National Park suitable for an all-terrain pushchair. There are both circular and "there-and-back" routes, and many can be shortened or have worthwhile detours. Walks range from half a mile to 6½ miles in length and cover a wide range of difficulty which we hope will cater for all types of walkers. The walks encompass both coastal and inland areas, so, hopefully, you will find a suitable walk nearby, wherever you are. The walks are not exhaustive and are intended as an introduction to the area. There are many other suitable routes to explore once you know what is possible with a pushchair.

Routes and Grades

We have purposefully made this book as easy to follow as possible. Each walk is accompanied by a simple route map showing the start point and numbers referring to details in the text, as well as obvious features. The maps are intended to be used in conjunction with the relevant Ordnance Survey Explorer map, and the information on them is by no means comprehensive. Details of the relevant map and the starting grid reference are given in the walk summary.

Each walk contains an "at-a-glance" key which tells you all you need to know to prepare for the walk – distance, difficulty, any stiles, facilities such as toilets or ice cream vans and any hidden costs, so there shouldn't be any nasty surprises when you set off. You can also see whether the walk requires two people to overcome obstacles or if it can be accomplished solo.

The walks have a basic summary, detailing points of interest and useful information on the area. We have also included an "in the area" section, suggesting nearby alternative activities for yourself and your family.

You should always allow more time than that recommended. Times given are approximate and based on a speed of two miles an hour. However, not everyone walks at the same speed and the times given do not make allowances for picnics, tantrum breaks or walking toddlers.

It should be noted that circular routes are written in the direction which requires the least effort and are not always reversible! If you are thinking of reversing a walk, read the description carefully to check it is possible.

Fitness

It is assumed that walkers will have a basic level of fitness. Those who consider themselves unfit should only attempt the easiest level of walk and, if necessary, take advice from their doctor. The hardest level of walk should only be attempted by those experienced in both walking and all-terrain pushchair technique.

All-Terrain Pushchairs – Advice for First-Time Buyers

There are now many makes of all-terrain pushchairs (ATPs) on the market. For help in choosing an ATP, here are some of the factors we have come across in researching this and other books!

Ensure your child is old enough for the ATP. Many makes have a reclining position suitable for use from birth, but bear in mind that very young babies should not be bumped around. Seek the manufacturer's advice and choose your walks carefully. Small babies (less than four months) should only be taken on the easiest level of walks and if you are not happy with the terrain, turn round!

Make sure the ATP has pneumatic tyres and good suspension to provide cushioning.

Lightweight prams are better!

Choose a long wheelbase, which makes leverage over obstacles easier than a short wheelbase. The front wheel should be fixed, or, at the very least, lockable. Rear wheels should be quick release.

Check the pushchair folds easily and that it fits in the boot of your car!

Shop around as it is always worth looking in the shops first and then checking the internet for the same pram at a better price – either new or used.

Accessories

A rain cover is essential, especially when out walking in the hills as the weather can change very quickly. Good quality footmuffs are easily available, if not already included in the price; fleece-lining and/or windproofing provides extra comfort.

Sunshades supplement the hood, which generally doesn't extend enough for walking uphill into full sun. Mesh shades are easier to walk with than parasols.

A puncture repair kit and pump are strongly advisable for those emergency situations. You can also fill the tyres with a "goo" designed as an emergency fix for bicycle tyres and which prevents serious deflation.

We've found a pram leash useful, especially on walks with steep drops or steep descents. This is a strap, climbing sling or piece of rope tied to the pram handle and fastened to the wrist. This provides extra security should you accidentally let go of the pushchair, and is more secure than a handbrake.

Single and Double All-Terrain Pushchairs from the 'Mountain Buggy' range. *Reproduced by permission of Chariots All-Terrain Pushchairs www.pushchairs.co.uk*

What to take

For the baby:

✻ Pram with rain cover, sun cover, footmuff and puncture repair kit.

✻ Milk – if you are not

breastfeeding, formula milk is easily carried in ready made cartons or powder sachets, then just add to water in bottles when you need it. If your baby likes warm milk, either carry warm water in a flask or make up extra hot milk and wrap in foil or a muslin.

* Nappies, wipes and nappy bag.

* Picnic – sandwiches are easy if your baby eats on his/her own, otherwise take fruit pots, yoghurt or anything easy to open. Don't forget a spoon and take all rubbish home with you.

* Snacks to cheer up a bored or peckish baby until you find a picnic spot. We have found that raisins or baby crisps keep them occupied for the longest!

* Water/juice

* Spare clothes. Layers are best as they can easily be put on or taken off as conditions change. Don't forget that though you may be hot walking uphill, your baby is sat still in the pushchair. Keep checking he/she is not too cold. An all in one fleece is a good buy. Look for one with fold-over ends to keep hands and feet warm – easier than gloves.

* Hat, either a sunhat or woolly hat depending on the weather conditions.

* Shoes for when your little one wants to get out.

For you

* Appropriate shoes (check the guide at the start of the walk) and coat. Keep a light waterproof in the pram ready for emergencies.

* Food and drink: it's very easy to forget your own in the rush to pack your baby's feast!

* Mobile phone.

* Small first aid kit.

* This guidebook and the relevant Ordnance Survey map for the walk.

The Countryside Code

* ✻ Respect – Protect – Enjoy
* ✻ Do not drop litter. Use a bin or take it home.
* ✻ Do not stray from public footpaths or bridleways.
* ✻ Do not pick any plants.
* ✻ Make no unnecessary noise.
* ✻ Keep dogs on a lead near livestock and under close control at all other times.
* ✻ Leave gates as you find them.
* ✻ Use gates or stiles to cross fences, hedges or walls.
* ✻ Do not touch livestock, crops or farm machinery.
* ✻ Keep the natural water supply clean.
* ✻ Walk in single file and on the right-hand side of roads.
* ✻ Do not cross railway lines except by bridges.
* ✻ Guard against the risk of fire.
    For information on new access rights, visit www.countysideaccess.gov.uk or phone 0845 100 3298.

Why walk?

* ✻ Walking makes you feel good
* ✻ Walking reduces stress
* ✻ Walking helps you see more of your surroundings
* ✻ Walking helps you return to your pre-pregnancy figure and......
* ✻ Walking helps your baby learn about his/her surroundings and nature

The North York Moors

The North York Moors National Park is an area of outstanding beauty and varied terrain 30 miles north of York stretching from Thirsk to the coast. It has the largest expanse of heather moorland in England, which is a stunning purple in summer and hums with the sound of bees as they gather pollen to make the area's famous heather honey. The coastal region has breathtaking cliffs with historic fishing villages nestling in coves at the base of steep-sided, wooded valleys. Add to this rolling hills, hidden waterfalls, grassy dales and picturesque villages and you've got a pretty good place to go walking!

Given the varied terrain it is a surprisingly good area for pushchair walking due to the extensive network of bridleways criss-crossing the countryside. The area is popular with horse riders, therefore, these bridleways are generally well maintained with easy access gateways at field boundaries.

We've chosen a selection of walks to show you the variety of scenery on offer as well as a variety of difficulties! The walks range from coastal strolls to riverside rambles to a grand and strenuous tour around Roseberry Topping. The area is also rich in legend and history, which we've tried to cover to some extent in the walk locations. Whichever you choose, you will certainly appreciate the stunning beauty of the Moors.

The walks are across moorland and farmland, along coastal paths and through forestry on a combination of public rights of way, forest tracks and access paths. Rights of way on access paths and access land are at the discretion of the landowner as defined under the Countryside and Rights of Way Act 2000, and though all routes are allowed at time of writing, permission could potentially be withdrawn in the future.

Routes along beaches and some coastal sections are affected by tides. If a walk is tide-dependent we have mentioned this in the introduction and an alternative, there-and-back route is possible. Always check the tide as on some walks it is possible to be cut off part way across a coastal section. Tide tables are available in most outdoor shops and tourist information centres. Many national newspapers publish tide times and heights (usually on the weather page) or they can be checked on www.britishinformation.com or www.bbc.co.uk/weather/coast/tides/.

When crossing farmland, always pay due consideration to livestock. Keep dogs on a lead, older children under control and never disturb any animal you come across. In addition, herds of cows can be problematic and have (fortunately rarely) been known to kill humans by stampeding. We have known cows to be particularly interested in the pushchair! If you are in any doubt as to your safety, leave the field by the nearest possible exit and abandon the walk.

Heather moorland is very susceptible to fire. During the summer months fires are very easily started in the dry heather and once started can burn for months on the peaty soils causing vast areas of devastation. Make sure you don't drop matches, cigarettes or glass and don't light camp fires or barbecues.

Always remember the weather can change very rapidly and there can be few landmarks if fog descends! Make sure you are equipped for all conditions and if in doubt turn back and return the way you came.

Transport

Finally, a few useful facts to help you on your way. The area is well served by public transport with the Moorsbus; a network of buses covering the national park and visiting the main tourist destinations. The service runs from April to the end of October running every Sunday and Bank Holiday and daily during the school summer holidays. Some services also run on weekdays from June. The bus is cheap and ideal if you want to do a one-way walk or just want to be green! Information and timetables are available at information centres, on www.moor.uk.net/moorsbus or by phoning 01845 597000. Other local buses also run between the main towns (0870 6082608).

In addition, the North Yorkshire Moors Railway runs from Pickering in the south to Grosmont in the north of the area with some connecting mainline services to Whitby. The Esk Valley mainline runs from Whitby to Middlesborough allowing access to the north of the area.

Circular route.

There and back. Route is non-circular.

Easy route with very few hills.

Moderate exertion. Some gentle ascents and descents.

Hard going. Route incorporates some steep inclines.

Easy terrain, trainers suitable.

Muddy and wet. Wellington boots or hiking boots are required.

Rough terrain. Rocky and uneven ground, hiking boots recommended.

Stile

Icecream van on route!

Tea shop.

Pub/Hotel.

Picnic table.

Children's play ground

Trains.

Ducks!

Toilets.

Solo. Walk can be accomplished alone.

At least two people required to complete walk. Pushchair may need to be lifted over obstacles.

Money required for parking, entrance fee or rail fare.

Walk 1: Sutton Bank and the White Horse, Kilburn

Allow: 1 hour 30 minutes

Sutton Bank is a high limestone escarpment at the very edge of the North York Moors with stunning views over the Vales of York and Mowbray. Because of its location and high elevation, Sutton Bank is home to the Yorkshire Gliding Club and on a clear day you can watch the gliders take off and land.

This walk takes you along the edge of Whitestonecliffe and Roulston Scar to Kilburn White Horse, a Victorian hill figure cut into the hillside. The path is very easy going and the route is actually designated an easy access route.

Map: Ordnance Survey 1:25000 Explorer OL26 – grid reference 514830

Distance: 3 miles (4.8km)

Getting there: Sutton Bank is on the A170 between Thirsk and Helmsley. The National Park Centre is located at the top of Sutton Bank; park in the main car park (fee). (N.B. Caravans, coaches and HGVs are banned on the bank and must follow the signposted alternative route if heading from the Thirsk direction). The M2 bus also stops at the Park Centre.

From the car park, go past the visitor centre following the signposted trail "Window on the Park".

There are information boards on wildlife and plants in the area as you walk around the National Park Centre.

1. When you get to the picnic site, go past it and straight across the second car park to the main road. Cross the road very carefully as it is busy! Continue along the path on the other side of the road. At the fork in the path, turn left.

The right-hand fork takes you to a telescope viewing point for a

Walking along Whitestonecliffe

more detailed look at the spectacular views across the plain to the west. This path loops round to meet up with the main path.

Walk along the level path that follows the top of the limestone escarpment, Whitestonecliffe, keeping children under control as there is a very big drop to your right!

The rocks here are Jurassic limestone, which formed in a shallow, tropical sea between 183 and 150 million years ago. This limestone stretches all the way to the coast around Scarborough and many fossils can be found.

Pass the memorial to allied air crews, and look out for gliders taking off from the airfield to your left.

Behind you is the isolated Lake Gormire, the only natural lake in the National Park and which is rumoured to be bottomless! There are many folk tales associated with the lake, one of which tells of a knight who tricked the Abbot of Rievaulx into lending him his white mare, but the horse would not obey the knight's commands. As he

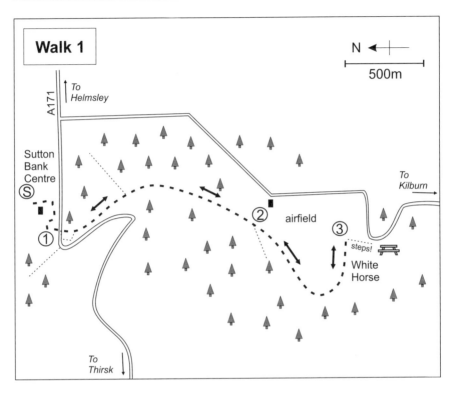

rapidly approached the cliff edge, he heard a sinister laugh and turned to see the Abbot who had turned into the devil. The knight plunged over the cliff into Lake Gormire. In reality, the lake originally formed in a glacial outwash channel, which carried meltwater into the large glacial lakes, which typified the area. These days the lake has no influx or outflow from rivers and sits in the middle of a large landslip, which sealed the southern end of the original channel. It is a breeding place for coot, great crested grebe and mallard.

2. Continue past the airfield and at the path junction carry on straight ahead along the top of the scarp. At the end of the limestone promontory, just at the end of the airfield, you are rewarded with spectacular views across most of Yorkshire! The village of Kilburn is directly below you at the foot of the high cliffs.

Kilburn's most famous resident is a furniture maker known as the

Mouseman. Born in 1876, Robert Thompson was a fine carpenter and woodworker who became known all over the world. He taught himself to use traditional woodworking tools and produced his own designs for furniture based on the styles of the 17th century. Every piece he carved features an unobtrusive little mouse. The origin of the mouse comes from his first commission, to carve the pews and rood screen at Hubberholme Church in Wharfedale, when he was as poor as a church mouse. Today examples of his craftsmanship can be found throughout Yorkshire including Beverley Minster and Ripon Cathedral.

Follow the path as it follows the top of Roulston Scar to the left, until you reach the top of the white horse, which is marked by white fencing.

Kilburn White Horse (314' long and 228' high) was cut in 1857 by the local schoolmaster, John Hodgson, and several helpers. It was designed and funded by Thomas Taylor, who was born in Kilburn. Taylor decided Yorkshire should have its own white horse after visiting the famous Uffington horse in Berkshire. As the rock here is limestone, not chalk, the horse needs to be whitened to make it stand out from the hillside. Originally, this was done by painting with whitewash, but these days, chalk chippings are used. Walking on the horse is prohibited.

3. If you're feeling very energetic (or just desperate for an ice cream!) you can head down the steps to the lower car park, where there is a nice grassy area for a play and a lower view of the white horse. Unfortunately, you do have to return up the steps!

   If you're not feeling energetic, just head back the way you came until you get to the visitor centre and your car.

In the area:

Monk Park Farm near Kilburn (www.monkpark.co.uk) is a farm visitor centre offering animal feeding, walks around the farm and lake, picnic and play areas and a tea room. As well as the usual farm animals, you'll also see chinchillas, wallabies and rhea! Open March to October.

The Mouse Man Visitor Centre (www.robertthompsons.co.uk) in Kilburn lies beneath the White Horse and offers an insight into the woodcraft started by Robert Thompson, the Mouse Man, and continued today by skilled craftsmen. His home is preserved as an example of a 16th-century cottage; you can view the craftsmen at work or walk in the gardens where you get stunning views of the surrounding countryside. Café and shop. Open Easter – September.

Walk 2: Hambleton Road, Kepwick to Boltby Forest

Allow: *1 hour 30 minutes*

This is a lovely walk across the top of heather moorland and through a pleasant forestry commission plantation. The views are excellent throughout and the paths are wide and even.

The Hambleton Hills lie at the western edge of the North York Moors and the Hambleton Drove Road runs along their crest. This road was part of an ancient highway between Scotland and the south of England. It is thought to date from prehistoric times but was heavily used in the 18th and 19th centuries by nomadic cattle drovers who moved their animals from Scotland to the markets of London. Cattle, sheep, pigs and geese were once all driven along the road but the advent of the railways meant that this was no longer necessary and the road went out of use in the early 20th century.

The route also takes you through the coniferous plantation of Boltby Forest. Roe and fallow deer, badgers and foxes all frequent this forest so keep your eyes open especially on early morning or evening walks.

Map: Ordnance Survey 1:25000 Explorer OL26 – grid reference 489915

Distance: 3 miles (4.8km)

Getting there: From the village of Kepwick take the road marked 'unsuitable for motor vehicles' up towards the moors. This road passes to the left of Kepwick Hall. Go through two gates and park your car on the left-hand side next to the wall immediately after the second gate. There is a Cleveland Way signpost and an information point at this site.

Walk along the Cleveland Way in the direction of Sutton Bank with the wall to your right. This is a broad dirt track through heather moorland.

There are fantastic views to your right over Kepwick, Osmotherley and beyond!

Boltby Forest ...!

1. Turn right through the gateway marked with a blue bridleway arrow onto a broad grassy path.

   The views from this path are very impressive on a clear day. If you look directly below you to the base of the hill you will be able to see Kepwick Hall.

2. The path bears round to the left and towards Boltby Forest. Go through the gateway before the forest and turn immediately left following the dry stone wall. Turn left onto a large track and follow this into the forest.

3. Follow this track up hill and through to the other side of the forest. Stay on the same track until you see a barrier ahead. Turn left immediately after the barrier and go through the gateway.

   The remains of Steeple cross, one of 30 named stone crosses on the North York Moors, lie just off the drovers road to the right of the gateway. Only the shaft of the cross is present and on this is carved CT1700 referring to Charles Tancred, Lord of the Manor of Arden Hall.

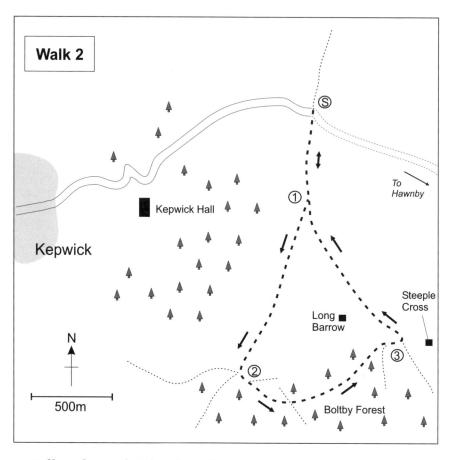

Follow the track (Cleveland Way) straight ahead keeping the wall to your left. Simply stay on this track until you find your car.

To the left of the wall is the site of a long barrow burial mound. This is one of the few New Stone Age (4300 -2000BC) barrows on the moors.

In the area:

Big Sheep and Little Cow Farm, Bedale (www.farmattraction.co.uk) is a family run attraction. You are guided round the farm and can help feed the animals, bath a pig and talk to the donkeys. There is also an indoor play area where parents can relax with a coffee and pastry. Pony rides and quad bikes are also on offer for the more adventurous. Open all year, check for seasonal times.

Rievaulx Abbey (www.english-heritage.org.uk) was founded in 1132 and was the first Cistercian Abbey in northern England. Today it is in ruins but you can still see the impressive scale of the site and learn how monastic life changed over the years. The nearby Rievaulx Terrace and Temples (National Trust) is a splendid 18th-century landscaped garden with stunning views over the Abbey and the nearby Hambleton Hills. Perfect for a leisurely stroll and a picnic.

Walk 3: Newgate Bank and Rievaulx Moor

Allow: *2 hours 30 minutes*

This is a fantastic walk along the edge of Rievaulx Moor, looking down into Bilsdale, and then back through Newgate Bank Plantation. There are lovely views across the moors, the Vale of Pickering and the Hambleton Hills and plenty of opportunities for a picnic in the heather in good weather.

Most of the route is on good forestry tracks, but there are steep gradients at either end of the bank. Gradients can be avoided to make this an easy route simply by walking to the trig point and back, still well worth the walk.

Map: Ordnance Survey 1:25000 Explorer OL26 – grid reference 563890

Distance: 4½ miles (7.2km)

Getting there: From the B1257 between Chop Gate and Helmsley, park in the Newgate Bank forestry commission car park. Toilets and picnic tables in the car park. Toilets are closed in the winter.

Walk back to the car park entrance and turn left down a broad track marked as a public footpath.

1. Leave the trees at an information board and continue along the track.

   You now walking on Rievaulx Moor, a patch of high moorland typical of the North York Moors with its dense heather cover and steep escarpment down into the valleys to the north. The heather is a stunning purple when in bloom in autumn and you can almost smell the honey!

   Continue along the track looking down into Bilsdale to your left, ignoring paths across the moors to your right. Go past a path down to your left (Ayton Bank) and continue along the track.

Newgate Bank

Look out for grouse and pheasants and, if you're lucky, you may see other birds as the moors are a nesting habitat for curlew, lapwing and plover.

Continue past the path down Rievaulx Bank to your left until you reach the trig point (328m), which is the highest point of Rievaulx Moor. Turn back here if you're opting for the flat there-and-back route!

On a clear day there are marvellous panoramic views from the trig point across to Helmsley and Pockley Moors ahead, down into Bilsdale to your left and across to the Hambleton Hills back the way you came.

2. To do the full circuit, continue past the trig point along the track until you reach the road on Helmsley Bank, where there are two benches to sit on and take in the views. Turn left onto the road to walk down the steep hill.

You could leave a car here if you wanted to do the walk one way.

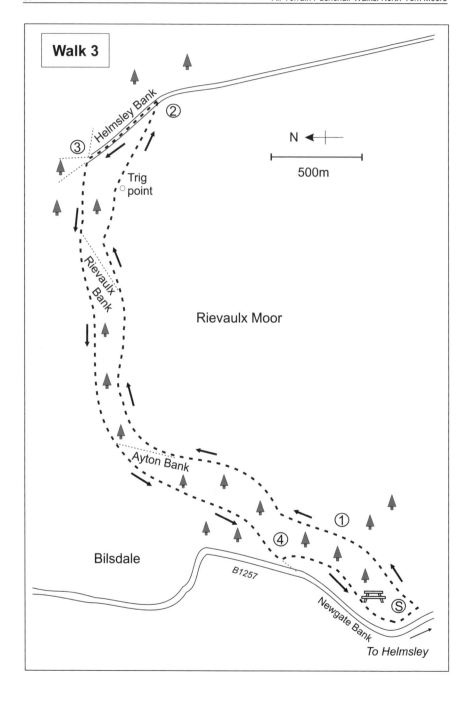

Walk 3

Helmsley Bank

②

③

Trig
point

N

500m

Rievaulx
Bank

Rievaulx Moor

Ayton Bank

Bilsdale

B1257

①

④

Newgate Bank

S

To Helmsley

3. At the end of the metalled road, there is a junction with several forest tracks. Take the first left-hand track marked by a bridleway sign – don't go down the track signposted to Potter House Farm.

Continue along the obvious forestry track, ignoring smaller paths to the left and right until the road comes into view.

From here you get good views down into Bilsdale, which were partially obscured by the trees from the top.

4. Before you reach the road, there is a path uphill to the left, marked as a bridleway. This is the crux of the walk!! Turn up the path, which is steep for about 20m before the incline decreases slightly. Continue the slog uphill for about 200m. Where the track levels off, take the right-hand turn and continue along this path, past the stone observation tower back to the car park.

In the area:

Bilsdale Riding Centre, (01439 798225) offers rides around the plethora of local bridleways and green lanes. Rides can last for 1 hour, half day or whole day. Riding hats are provided but stout shoes (not trainers) are required.

Helmsley Castle, (www.english-heritage.org.uk) is a 13th-century castle built on the site of an earlier wooden castle. The impressive double ditch is the only remnant of the original castle and the stone replacement has an unusual D-shaped keep. The castle was damaged and abandoned during the Civil War and the ruins provide a fun place to explore. Open all year.

Walk 4: St Gregory's Minster and Kirkdale Hyena Cave

Allow: *1 hour 30 minutes*

This is a beautiful walk that takes you along a secluded wooded valley to the ancient church of St Gregory's Minster. The Minster was built between 1055 and 1065 from the remains of an even older church. It is of historical interest as the inscription above the door is the longest surviving example of Anglo Saxon carving and gives a very accurate date for the building of the church.

There is also the option to see Kirkdale Hyena Cave, which caused a sensation in the 19th century due to the vast quantities of bones found in the cave. The cave is part way up a limestone cliff and not easily accessible, but it is easily visible from the path.

N.B. The route crosses a river bed near St. Gregory's Minster. This section of the river is dry for most of the year, as the river flows underground, but if there have been heavy rains it is recommended that you check that this section is passable before you start.

Map: Ordnance Survey 1:25000 Explorer OL26 – grid reference 676856

Distance: 2½ miles (4km)

Getting there: Take the turning to St Gregory's Minster from the A170 between Nawton and Kirkbymoorside. Park in the lay-by next to the turning down to the church car park.

At the lay-by and road junction you will see a signposted bridleway marked Inn Way (on your left when you are facing down towards the church). Take this narrow path up the bank and through the gateway at the top into a field.

Turn right and follow the field boundary. Go through a gateway and continue walking along the right-hand edge of the field to a further gateway in view ahead. This gateway takes you onto a narrow trail through broadleaved and conifer woodland.

St Gregory's Minster

1. At the end of the woodland path you will come to a road. Turn right and walk down this quiet no-through road.

   You will pass an old lime kiln on the left of the road. Be aware of the steep slope on the right-hand side of the road if you have toddlers.

2. The road eventually brings you to an old mill on Hodge Beck at Hold Caldron. Cross over the beck at a stone bridge and turn immediately right through a gateway.

   Follow the path as it bears left up the hill through the broadleaved and conifer woodland. At the fork in the path turn right onto the level path. Don't go on the left-hand path, which continues up the hill.

   The broad path gradually descends down the hill with Hodge Beck on the right. Continue following the path (yellow marker with blue arrow) as it heads away from the beck for a short while.

   The path narrows and goes past a large meadow on the right. There is a short very narrow section of path with some tree roots to negotiate. However, the path soon opens out again and goes back into the woodland.

Go through another gateway and then another path joins ours from the left. Simply continue straight ahead until you come to a fork in the path. Follow the track on the right down to the beck (marked with a blue arrow in a yellow circle).

Go through a meadow and follow the path across the beck. There used to be a footbridge here but it is lying in ruin nearby! The river bed is dry for most of the year and so there is usually no problem crossing it. However, it may be easier to carry the push-chair over.

3. Once you have crossed the beck follow the path to St Gregory's Minister which you will be able to see ahead. Go through the gate and the church is on your left. Once you have finished at the church, follow the path up the road and back to your car in the lay-by.

The inscription above the door is the longest surviving example of Anglo Saxon carving and translates as:

"Orm son of Gamal bought St Gregory's Minster when it was all broken and fallen, and he caused it to be made anew from the ground, for Christ and St Gregory, in the days of King Edward and in the days of Earl Tosti and Hawarth wrought me and Brand the Prior. This is sun's marker at all times".

The Edward referred to is Edward the Confessor, (1042-1066) and Tostig was the Earl of Northumberland in 1055 and Harold Godwinson's brother. Hawarth was the craftsman who made the sundial. All that remains of Orm's original church are the south, west and east walls of the nave, the archway in the west wall of the nave (which probably formed the original entrance) and the jambs, angle-shafts, bases and capitals of the arch which leads from the nave into the chancel.

If you want to go and see the entrance to the Hyena cave turn left

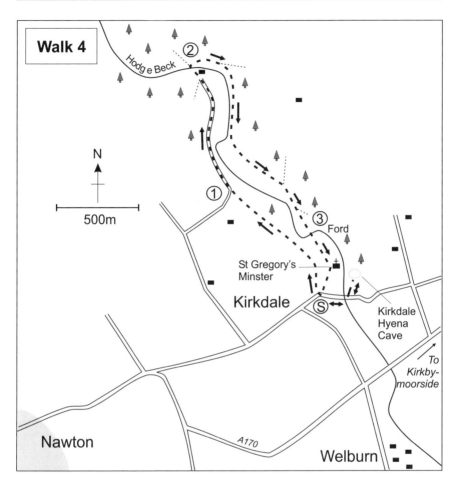

at the end of the church road and follow the lane down the hill. Turn left to cross over a small footbridge. Take the second path on the left after the bridge, which takes you into the woodland. Follow the path as it bears round to the right. You will soon come to a rocky crag in which you will see a small cave opening.

The cave here was discovered by quarrymen and first explored in 1821. It revealed a treasure trove of archaeological remains including Stone Age tools and the bones of elephants, rhinos, hippos, lion, tiger, bison, wolf, horse, deer, bear and the remains of almost 300 hyenas! The bones were identified by William Buckland,

Professor of Geology at Oxford, who suggested the cave had been a hyena den where the animals had dragged their prey to be eaten. Buckland also attested that the bones were proof of the biblical flood. While this may seem amusing today, the animal remains present do show that the climate here was much warmer in the Stone Age and that global warming is not just a new or man-made phenomenon!

Retrace your steps to get back to your car.

In the area:

Duncombe Park, Helmsley (www.duncombepark.com) is a stunning historic house set in acres of beautiful gardens and parkland. The home of Lord and Lady Feversham, the house offers grand rooms and you are welcome to walk, picnic and play in the gardens and parkland. There is a small adventure playground to entertain the children and shopping, food and drink for the grown-ups. Open end April to end October 11-5.30.

Flamingoland, (www.flamingoland.co.uk) between Pickering and Malton, is a famous theme park with classic rides, exotic bird shows, Muddy Duck Farm for the under 10's and a collection of wild animals from hippos and lions to meerkats and sea lions. It's pricey but guaranteed to fill a whole day! Open April to October.

Walk 5: The Daffodils Walk, River Dove, Farndale

Allow: *2 hours*

This walk takes you along part of the picturesque valley of Farndale and is beautiful all year round. However, it is especially good in March and April when the wild daffodils, for which the valley is famous, are in bloom and which carpet the riverbanks. Though reputedly planted by monks from Rievaulx Abbey, the daffodils are truly wild. They are the *Narcissus pseudonarcissus* species and smaller and more delicate than cultivated species, with half-nodding flowers and a 'trumpet' of slightly darker yellow than the petals.

This is a very easy walk along level, well maintained paths. Mid-April is normally the time to see the daffodils at their best, though they flower from March to early May. The daffodils are protected by law, so make sure no-one tries to pick them.

Map: Ordnance Survey 1:25000 Explorer OL26 – grid reference 672952

Distance: 2¾ miles (4.4km)

Getting there: Park in the car park at Low Mill. There are toilets in the car park.

The Daffodil bus runs during flowering season and is a 15-minute shuttle bus from Hutton-le-Hole every Sunday until April 30 as well as Easter weekend.

Take the signposted public path to High Mill from the car park. This takes you through a gateway and down the path to a second gateway ahead. Go through the gate and cross the footbridge over the River Dove. Turn left through a gate and walk along the path with the river on your left.

About now, in spring you should start to see the daffodil displays. There are also lovely views over Low Blakey Moor to your right.

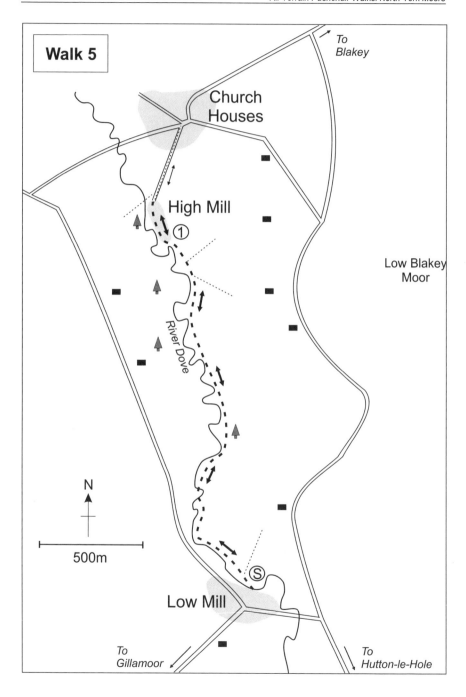

Walk 5

Church
Houses

To
Blakey

High Mill

①

Low Blakey
Moor

River Dove

N

500m

Low Mill

To
Gillamoor

To
Hutton-le-Hole

The path follows the course of the river and passes through meadows and woodland. You will pass through eleven gates along the route.

1. Eventually you will see the buildings at High Mill ahead. Pass through a final gate and into the village. You will find the Daffy Café in the village on the right. There is an outside seating area with a children's playground and they have a high chair and toilets. Ice creams are also on sale here!

The Daffy Café is open every day in March and April and Friday to Sunday in February and from May to September.

If you continue up the lane you will soon come to Church Houses where there is a pub (Feversham Arms) which has a beer garden. When you have had refreshments, return to your car along the route you came.

In the area:

At **Ryedale Folk Museum** in Hutton-le-Hole you can explore 19 historic buildings and discover how our ancestors lived. Each building shows a different aspect of rural life from the humble peasant to the lord of the manor and ranging in time from Mediaeval to the 20th century. Shop, pub, café and picnic areas. Dogs welcome on a lead. Open all year 10am – 5.30pm (www.ryedalefolkmuseum.co.uk).

Byland Abbey (www.english-heritage.org.uk), near Helmsley is a lovely ruin and the home to the largest collection of in situ mediaeval floor tiles in Europe. It was founded in 1134 and is one of three main abbeys in North Yorkshire. The monks were particularly known for their sheep and the export of wool. The remains include one of the largest cloisters in England, stunning 13th-century floor tiles in the church, and the only stone lectern base in England.

Walk 6: Rosedale Iron Mining Trail

Allow: 2 hrs

This is an easy walk and you can go as far as you want as you simply return along the same route. The walk takes you along the old Iron Railway to Sherriff's Pit, a disused mine shaft on the western rim of Rosedale. Along the route you can see the ruins of a once thriving iron mining area, with remains visible on both sides of the valley. The route of the level tramway used to transport the iron ore can still be followed right around the head of the valley and makes an ideal pushchair path! You can explore the mine ruins and there are excellent views over the East Rosedale mines and across the Rosedale valley so don't forget to pack your binoculars!

The walk takes you through heather moorland which is an internationally important territory for ground nesting birds including golden plover and merlin and the nationally important curlew, lapwing and nightjar.

N.B. As this is an old mining area, there are open shafts and adits at the surface. Take extreme care to stay on the footpath and keep children and animals under strict control. Do not cross any fencing

Map: Ordnance Survey 1:25000 Explorer OL26 – grid reference 722950

Distance: 4 miles (6.5km)

Getting there: Park in the lower Chimney Bank car park (next to the Iron Kilns) on the road from Hutton-le-Hole to Rosedale Abbey.

Walk along the gravel track from the car park which passes to the right of the Iron Kilns.

The kilns are the first evidence you come across of the old workings of the Rosedale West mines. Though there has been evidence of

Kilns at Rosedale West Mines

small-scale iron workings from Mediaeval times, mining escalated in 1857 when the West mines were opened to exploit a ore deposit containing a whopping 49% of iron (most ores contain around 30%). The kilns here were built to process the ore by calcining, a heating process to remove water, volatiles and sulphur from the ore. Processing on site reduced the weight and hence cost of transporting the ore to the blast furnaces in Middlesborough. The iron ore here is magnetic, so don't rely on your compass as the needle will be affected by the rocks beneath your feet!

The track shortly joins onto a broad track from the left. Continue straight ahead with the valley of Rosedale to your right.

The broad dirt and stone track you are walking along is the bed of a dismantled railway built to transport the increasing quantities of ore to Teesside. When the mines first opened, the ore was transported by road to Pickering to the south, but in 1858 the existing North Yorkshire and Cleveland Railway extended its line to include the mines. They even built a siding for the farmers living in

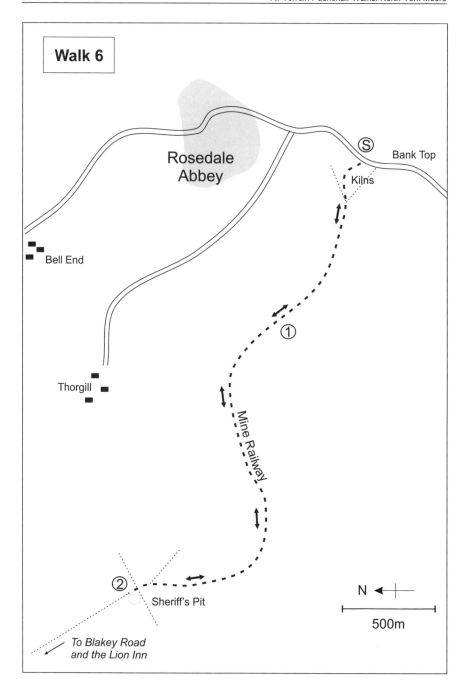

Walk 6

Rosedale
Abbey

Bank Top

Ⓢ

Kilns

Bell End

①

Thorgill

Mine Railway

②

Sheriff's Pit

*To Blakey Road
and the Lion Inn*

N

500m

nearby Farndale! The ruins of an engine house and chimney can be found on the left of the railway track just before the junction with the gravel track from the kilns. The 100ft chimney at Bank Top was a local landmark until it was demolished in 1972.

1. As you walk along you go past a barrier and soon you will see stones from a previous mining building on the right and a lovely carved bench which is a perfect place to admire the views.

There are fantastic views along the length of Rosedale to your right. You will soon be able to see the village of Rosedale Abbey in the bottom of the valley. Though hard to believe today, the valley was home to a thriving mining industry with around 3000 inhabitants at its peak in 1871. Many of the rows of cottages you can see in the valley below were built to house the workers and their families.

2. Continue along this track for 2km until you come to the remains of a building and a fenced off pit on your left.

This is Sheriff's Pit, a 270ft deep vertical shaft with horizontal adits into the hillside below, one of which extends for 1500ft to the shaft bottom. Look for the remains of Rosedale East Mines on the opposite side of the valley from this point. The East Mines opened slightly later, in 1859, and produced over 300,000 tonnes of ore in their heyday in the early 1870's. The mines were operational until 1926 following a general strike, after which the mine never re-opened.

This is the turning point for the walk so return to your car along the same route.

It is possible to continue walking another 4km to a point where the old railway line meets Blakey Road (grid reference 683989). So if you are travelling in two or more cars you could leave a car in this car park and maybe pay a visit to the Lion Inn on Blakey Ridge!

In the area:

Ryedale Swimming Pool, Pickering (01751 473351) offers public swimming, parent and toddler sessions and fun sessions with slides and inflatables. Phone for session times.

York Castle Museum (www.yorkcastlemuseum.org) lets you learn all about Victorian life with real-life sounds, period lighting and Victorian characters in Kirkgate, a street complete with period shops and amusements. Pushchairs cannot be taken into the galleries but back packs and carrycots can be hired for free. Open all year 9.30am – 5pm.

Walk 7: Sinnington to Cropton Brewery

Allow: *2 hours 30 minutes*

This walk takes you from the tranquil village green in Sinnington across fields and through woodland to Cropton. The paths are good and even most of the way with only an occasional narrow section.

The rewards are great for reaching the half-way point for this walk, the New Inn and Cropton Brewery! This pub and microbrewery is a lovely place to stop for a bite to eat and to sample the local brew before returning along the same route. There's even a playground in the beer garden for the children!

The brewery (www.croptonbrewery.com; 01751 417330) runs daily tours between April and September from 11.30-2.30 but children under the age of 12 are not allowed into the brewery.

Map: Ordnance Survey 1:25000 Explorer OL27– grid reference 744858

Distance: 5 miles (8km)

Getting there: Take the Sinnington turning from the A170 between Kirbymoorside and Pickering. Park on the village green where there is an honesty box for parking fees.

Walk along the road with the River Seven on your immediate left and a stone bridge behind you. Next to a bench under a tree on your left you will see a signpost. Follow the bridleway and footpaths sign along the road to the right.

> The stone bridge that spans the River Seven behind you was built in the 18th century.

Follow the road as it bends to the left and then to the right in the direction of the church and the Hall. Pass All Saints Church and continue following the road in the direction of Hunters Hill.

Sinnington and the River Severn

At first sight All Saints just looks like a pretty Yorkshire village church but take a closer look at the stones with which this church was built! You can see that there are many pieces of pre-Norman crosses and hogback tombstones within the walls. These carved pieces of stone are scattered throughout the building both inside and out and are thought to come from a Saxon or Viking cemetery.

1. The path takes you past a large house (The Hall) and some out-buildings and the bridleway then bends to the left and takes you onto a track through a field.

   Continue along the track as it takes you past Stables Wood on the right and onto a path between two fields. The path narrows and takes you into Hob Bank Wood. The track can be bumpy and muddy in places and slightly overgrown in the summer. Stay on this path (Wiley Flat Lane), which takes you along the right-hand edge of the wood, ignoring tracks to the left.

   Turn right at a fork in the path and continue through the wood-

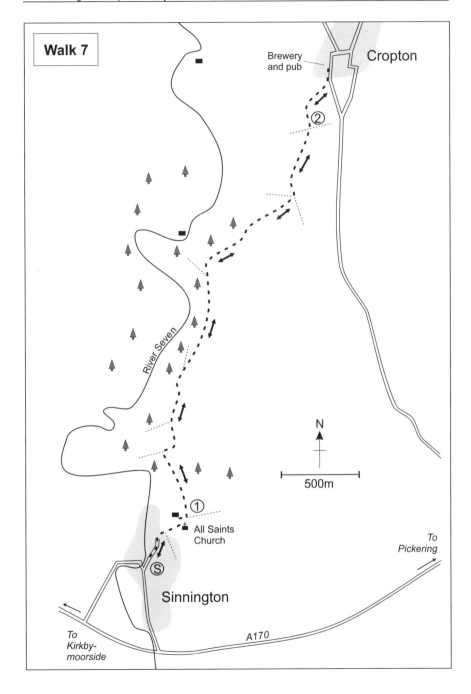

Walk 7

Brewery and pub

Cropton

River Seven

N

500m

All Saints Church

To Pickering

Sinnington

To Kirkby-moorside

A170

land to a gate. Pass through the gate and continue along the path ahead taking care of the steep drop to the left.

Go through a further gate and then through an open gateway. The path then forks and you must take the left-hand fork across the grass field.

2. At the next gate turn left onto a narrow path (Bull Ing Lane) between two hedges. The path broadens into a wide track after you pass a house on the left and eventually takes you to a lane (Cropton Lane).

Turn left into the village of Cropton and you will see the New Inn and Cropton Brewery ahead. The pub has a beer garden and family room with high chairs. There is also a church and craft shop in the village.

Brewing has been taking place in the village of Cropton since 1613 although in the early days it was strictly illegal! The current brewery was established in 1984 within the New Inn but has since moved to a new building on farmland behind the pub and now produces nine different beers.

This is the turning point for the walk so once you have visited the pub and brewery simply return to your car along the route you came.

In the area:

Castle Howard (www.castlehoward.co.uk), an award winning stately home and the setting of the TV series Brideshead Revisited, is one of England's most beautiful houses. Its stunning setting in extensive grounds between two lakes provides ample space for walking and the kids can let of steam in the adventure playground. Children's events and adventure trails are run during the holidays. The house also has a café, farm shop, plant nursery and gift shops. Open March to October.

Wyville Animal Farm in Slingsby, (01653 628333) is a working farm with a wide range of animals, kept in the traditional way. Visitors of all ages will find something to enjoy; you can cuddle and feed baby animals, visit the farm shop, relax in the coffee shop or buy local gifts in the gift shop. Open daily end-March to end-September 10.30am – 5pm.

Walk 8: Cawthorn Woods and Roman Camps, Cropton

Allow: *30 minutes*

This is an easy, flat walk through pleasant woodland to visit the remains of the Roman Camps at Cawthorn. All that can be seen today are earthworks, but the ramparts and ditches outlining the original structures are clearly visible. Major excavations in the 1920's established the site as being a series of temporary camps dating to the late 1st to early 2nd century AD. Later re-examination of the site suggested that it actually consisted of a single temporary camp and two forts, one of which had an annexe. The remains of turf-walled buildings have been seen in excavations and there is evidence of further inhabitation, possibly by Anglo-Saxons, as late as the 11th century. There have allegedly been strange sightings here at night....

The walk is well signposted from the car park and is a designated easy access trail indicating suitability for wheelchairs. The paths are easy gravel and grass and the route winds its way through pleasant woodland. There is a clearing with benches next to the car park for picnics and play time and it's a nice, short walk for those independent toddlers!

Map: Ordnance Survey 1:25000 Explorer OL27 – grid reference 782896

Distance: 1 mile (1.6km)

Getting there: Turn off the A170 at Wrelton and follow the signs to Cropton. Go past the New Inn pub and turn right into Cropton village (signposted). Follow the road round to the right. Pass a right turn to Cawthorn. 500m further on turn left down a forest road signposted to the Roman Camps. Park in the forest car park (no fee).

From the car park, walk towards the wooden signpost with a roman helmet. At the first fork in the path, turn right, following the arrow.

1. Go through the gate making note of the information that dogs must be kept under control and that adders and sheep may be on the site. Continue along the path.

The raised banks and ditch on your left are the remains of one of the roman camps here. Keep to the paths as the earthworks are easily damaged. This camp is thought to have been a practice camp and is unusual in that it is coffin-shaped. The Romans are thought to have practised their fort-building techniques here – rare evidence of the serious campaigning associated with occupation in this area and also with the building of Hadrian's Wall further north.

Continue along the edge of the camp through a clearing, and as you come back into the woods follow the Roman sign heading round to the right and into a second clearing. Ahead of you are the banks of another Roman Camp.

This is thought to have been a temporary camp, providing accommodation for the Romans as they worked on the other forts at the site. Across this feature (but inaccessible) is an adjoining structure, thought to have been an annexe.

2. Follow the path around to the left. Cross a wooden bridge and continue along the path, following it round to the left and past a bench with views across the moors to the north.

Continue to a clearing and a third camp. As you walk through the middle of this camp, the path changes abruptly from gravel to grass.

This is a typical Roman fort with double ditches, high ramparts and gateways in the centre of each rampart, which you pass through to walk across the fort. The rampart corners are typically rounded and evidence of buildings has been found within the ramparts.

3. Cross the fort and leave by the opposite gate. Turn right, to take advantage of a well-sited bench enjoying views to the north-west over Cropton Forest.

Cawthorn Woods – ideal for toddlers

When you've soaked up the view (and spotted the rain heading towards you!) head back to the path junction and continue straight ahead following the Roman helmet sign and continue as the path bears round to the right.

4. Go through the gate and continue through the woods until you reach a junction where you turn right (ignore the Roman sign – you've already walked up there!). Continue down the path until you reach the car park and your car.

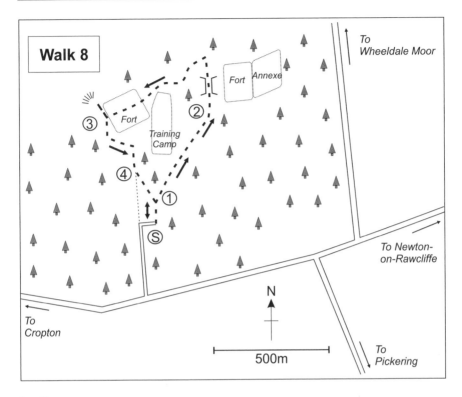

In the area:

Pickering Castle, (www.english-heritage.org.uk) is a Norman motte and bailey castle set within a deep moat. Cross the drawbridge to explore the ruined buildings, which date from the 12th century. Open all year.

Eden Camp (www.edencamp.co.uk) just outside Malton, is an award winning museum housed in what was once a prisoner of war camp. The exhibitions and reconstructions take you back through modern history to wartime Britain. There's a junior assault course to entertain the little ones, mess rooms to either eat a packed lunch or buy a meal and a baby changing and feeding room. Open all year 10am-5pm. No credit cards.

Walk 9: The Hole of Horcum and Skelton Tower

Allow: 3 hours 30 minutes

This is a long walk with fine views over moorland and valleys with plenty to see along the way. The walk begins at the Hole of Horcum, a vast ¼ mile hollow in the moorland, which is surrounded by legend. Some say that it was created by a twelve foot giant named Wade who lived at Mulgrave Castle (see walk 21). Wade and his wife, Bell, are said to have built both Mulgrave and Pickering Castles and whilst doing so they would share tools by throwing them back and forth between the two sites. On one occasion a hammer was thrown and did not reach its target but instead landed with such force that it created the Hole of Horcum. Other legends say that the hole was dug by the Devil when he grabbed a handful of earth to throw at his wife during an argument, the pile of earth forming Roseberry Topping (Walk 27). Hence the alternative name the Devil's Punchbowl. In truth Ice Age meltwaters and erosion from springs created the Hole of Horcum.

This walk could be cut short by simply walking out to Dundale Pond and back (5 miles) or turning back at any point before you reach the pond. This shortened walk gives great views of the Hole of Horcum but misses out Skelton Tower and Levisham Bottoms. Cutting the walk short would also avoid both the hills and the stiles.

Map: Ordnance Survey 1:25000 Explorer OL27 – grid reference 852936

Distance: 6½ miles (10.4km)

Getting there: Park in the Hole of Horcum car park, Saltergate on the A169 between Pickering and Sleights. There is a national park information point in this car park.

Cross over the road taking care for traffic, go down a few steps and turn right onto a narrow path. The Hole of Horcum is directly to your left.

At the point where the road takes a sharp right bend, follow the path through a large gateway. This takes you onto a broad, heather lined track along the top edge of the Hole of Horcum.

There are great views over the Hole of Horcum to your left and across heather moorland to your right.

1. After a long walk along this track (approximately 2 miles) you will arrive at Dundale Pond. If you wish to cut the walk short by 1½ miles then return along the route you came.

The valley around Dundale pond was given to the Monks of Malton in 1230 as pasture for their animals. It is thought that the pond was created at that time as a place for the animals to drink. Local folklore claims that this pond is bottomless.

To continue the walk to Skelton tower and Levisham Bottoms turn right immediately after the pond, signposted to 'The Station'. This narrow path goes through the bracken alongside the edge of the pond.

The path leads you to the corner of a dry stone wall where you must turn right, away from the wall. As you walk over the brow of the hill you will be able to see the ruins of Skelton Tower ahead. Follow the path as it takes you down the hill, across a crossroads and to the tower.

2. Turn left at the tower and follow the path through Levisham Bottoms.

Skelton Tower was built by the Rev Robert Skelton, vicar of Levisham, as a shooting lodge in 1850. The tower is a lovely place for a picnic and there are great views of the North York Moors Railway as it runs through the valley of Newtondale.

There are several criss-crossing paths along this route so pick you own route, keeping the hill to your right and the railway to your left.

Ahead you will be able to see the large early warning radar station at RAF Fylingdales.

Skelton Tower

3. After a long walk (approximately two miles) the path bears to the right and you will be able to see a white building ahead (The Saltergate Inn, a great place for refreshments with a play area!). Follow the path as it continues to bear right, go over a small spring and gradually walk uphill towards the road.

The Saltergate Inn was involved in salt smuggling during the salt tax years (1798-1825). The remote Inn provided the ideal location for Whitby fishermen to obtain smuggled salt supplies. It is said that the peat fire within the Inn has been burning for over 200 years and that it imprisons the spirit of a dead customs officer. After a failed raid on the Inn one of the customs officers returned alone at night to catch the smugglers. The officer was murdered that night and buried beneath the fireplace. It is said that if the fire ever goes out his spirit will awake and haunt the Inn.

The narrow path takes you to a stile. Lift the pushchair over and continue up the hill to a second stile. Turn immediately left through a gateway and follow the path back to the car park.

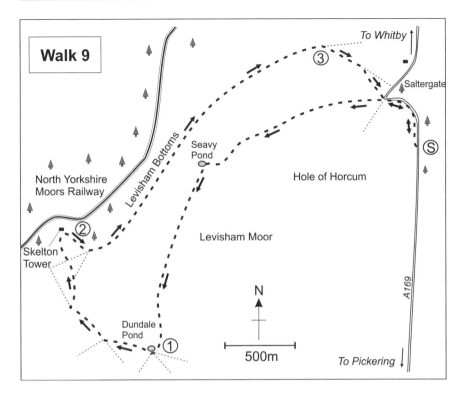

In the area:

Yorvik (www.vikingyorvik.com) is York's famous Viking museum and is located on the actual site where archaeologists discovered the remains of Yorvik, the Viking city. The museum takes you back 1000 years to see (and smell!) how the Vikings lived as you travel along reconstructed streets. Holographic talking "ghosts" take you round Viking artefacts, craftsmen recreate skills and you can have a go at an archaeological dig. Extra events during school holidays. Open all year. Phone 01904 543402 for a pre-booked time so you can jump the queue!

Wellington Lodge Llamas near Scarborough offers the opportunity to go llama trekking in some of the area's stunning scenery. Treks must be booked at least three days in advance. No dogs. (www.llamatreks.co.uk, 01723 871234)

Walk 10: Wheeldale Moor and Roman Road

Allow: 1 hour 30 minutes

Wheeldale Roman Road, originally known as Wade's Causeway, is one of the best preserved stretches of ancient roadway in Britain. It is built from large slabs, which form a mounded surface to help drainage. It was originally thought to have been built by the Romans to link Lees Rigg to the north with Cawthorn Camps (Walk 8) and the Roman garrison at Malton. However, the Roman origin is now less certain as there is no evidence of surface gravel, typical of Roman roads, and the road changes direction along its length; Roman roads were typically straight. It is now thought to either pre-date the Romans, or to have been built towards the end of the occupation when standards were slipping and when Saxons were invading the coast at Whitby. It is also thought to have been a trade route for transporting jet, a prized semi-precious stone, inland from the coast at Whitby.

The road cuts across a stretch of spectacular, isolated moorland which is vivid purple when the heather is in flower. Though an ancient road, the surface is not really suitable for pushchairs and should be avoided in order to protect the monument. This route follows a grassy path adjacent to the road before cutting across the hillside to meet the modern road a few hundred metres away.

N.B. The route-finding between the ancient and modern roads relies on good visibility. If visibility is poor, or if fog descends while you are out, either abandon the walk altogether or simply head back along the Roman road to ensure you don't get lost.

Map: Ordnance Survey 1:25000 Explorer OL27 – grid reference 973803

Distance: 2½ miles (4km)

Getting there: From the centre of Pickering, drive past the North Yorkshire Moors Railway station and continue along the road through Newbridge and Newton-on-Rawcliffe. Pass a left turn to Cropton and continue through Stape (scattered farms). Cross a ford and past forest onto Wheeldale Moor. Park in one of the lay-bys at Wheeldale Bridge (nice picnic spot by the stream!).

From Wheeldale Bridge, walk up hill to head through the gate next to an information board, following the Roman Road signpost. Once through the gate you are on the Roman Road. Follow the road, walking on the grass to the right of the road so as not to cause damage.

You can clearly see the road's structure with is a raised, gentle dome with stone banks to either side and large sandstone slabs on the surface. The road is also known as Wade's Causeway and legend has it that a giant called Wade built the road for his wife Bell to herd her sheep across the moor.

Continue next to the road, crossing the small drainage gulleys by the easiest route; many have stones placed for crossing.

If you're here in late summer when the heather is in flower the surrounding moorland turns a spectacular purple colour. If you stand quietly you can hear the buzzing of bees collecting the pollen to make delicious heather honey – highly recommended if you can find a jar!

Wade's Causeway

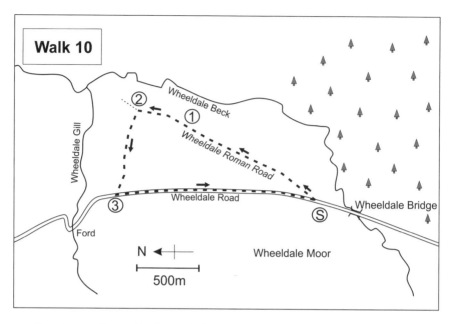

Continue along the line of the road, heading towards a gate in the wall.

Notice that the wall has actually been built over the road!

1. Go through the gate and continue along the road, which is now in a poorer condition and the route gets much bumpier so pick the best route you can amongst the stones. Keep heading towards a second wall and a gate.

2. Just before you get to the wall, turn sharp left to zig-zag back on yourself along a muddy, grassy track.

   N.B. The next section of route finding is tricky with few landmarks. If visibility is poor, turn back here and follow the Roman Road back to your car.

   Follow the wheel ruts until they peter out after about 25m, and then turn right, which takes you on a grassy path through heather and bracken. Continue along this path which will soon turn into a grassy track with well defined wheel ruts.

Head diagonally up the side of the hill. There should be a white caravan on the skyline to your left.

The path turns slightly left, heading steeper uphill. As the ground levels out, ignore the gate next to a white building and turn right heading parallel to this wall and towards a wall and gate in the distance.

3. Lift over the gate to join the road. Turn left and follow the road back to your car.

In the area:

Beck Isle Museum of Rural Life (www.beckislemuseum.co.uk) in Pickering shows the local life and customs of the past 200 years, and includes typical rooms, shops, workshops and farming equipment. Toilets and baby changing facilities. Open March to October.

The **Esk Valley Miniature Railway** in Ruswarp is a miniature steam railway (7.25 inch gauge) which runs for half a mile of landscaped track along the banks of the River Esk.

Walk 11: Goathland to Moorgates

Allow: 2 hours

This walk takes you through pretty countryside around the pictur-esque village of Goathland in the heart of the North York Moors. Goathland has been made famous in recent years as the setting for "Heartbeat" where it features as the village of Aidensfield. If you are familiar with the programme you will recognise the pub, garage/funeral directors and village shop, which all display their TV-set signage. You may even catch a glimpse of one of the stars!

The route runs alongside part of the North Yorkshire Moors Railway, and can be done as part of a day out on the train. The walk follows broad farm tracks, moorland paths and metalled roads. The paths can be quite muddy after wet weather, and there is a ford to cross, so wear good walking boots or wellies. It's also a good idea to take wellies for the children, as the puddles were very popular with our little walkers!

Map: Ordnance Survey 1:25000 Explorer OL27 – grid reference 836013

Distance: 3 miles (4.8km)

Getting there: Follow the A169 Pickering to Whitby road. Turn into Goathland and park in the village.
By Train: Take the North York Moors Railway to Goathland from Pickering or Grosmont.

From Goathland Station, go over the metal bridge and up the road into the village. Turn right just before the road junction to join the pavement and continue into the village until you reach the Goathland Hotel on your left.

Look out for the "Aidensfield Arms" sign on the side of the Goathland Hotel.

1. Turn left immediately after the hotel and over a cattle-grid (too widely spaced for toddler feet!) to follow a farm track. The track is

The North Yorkshire Moors Railway

signposted "Abbot's House Farm Campsite". Continue along the track until you reach the campsite.

At the cross-roads in the campsite continue straight ahead along the track marked with a signpost to Moorgates (blue arrow). Continue along the good farm track through broadleaved woodland.

Pass through a gate and continue along the track, now grassy, with glimpses of the North Yorkshire Moors Railway through the trees in the valley below. Continue straight on and through two more gates. Pass a farmhouse on your left and keep going towards a white gate. Pass a house on the right and go through the white gate to join the road at Moorgates.

Look out for the "Moor Crossing" sign on the garden fence. Across the road, you can also see evidence of a disused stretch of railway, as Moorgates marks the point where the present line splits from the original 1836 route of George Stephenson's Pickering to Whitby horse-drawn tramway. You can still see the railway embankment, gate-keeper's cottage and "Cattle Arch"; a bridge built to let cattle move freely between the coast and the Plain of York. Before the railway was built there were no obstacles to restrict such movement over the moors. This stretch of line was closed in 1865 when the new railway between Goathland and Grosmont was built, and which is the present route of the North Yorkshire Moors Railway.

2. Turn left and walk down the road, under the railway bridge and over a bridge across Eller Beck. Watch out for traffic! Though this is a small road it gets busy in summer.

The Gwyneth Paltrow film "Possession" was filmed on the railway here near Moorgates in 2000.

Pass a lay-by on your right (nice picnic spot on the river bank here!) and head up the hill until you reach a track heading off to the left, which is marked as a public bridleway.

Note the house sign for "Birchwood" at the start of the track – what's it made from??

Head along the track, past a memorial. As the track levels out there is a good view to the left across the railway to Two Howes Rigg, which is blanketed with purple heather in late summer.

3. Pass the left turn to Birchwood and bear right to continue along the bridleway. The bridleway is now a grassy track marked by a wooden post with a blue arrow to Goathland. This stretch of the route is quite rocky.

Head down hill to a gate. Pass through the gate to reach a ford. Push through the ford! You'll need wellies or high boots for this. (An alternative is to lift over the stepping stones but this is awkward and they can be slippy when wet.)

Pass a farm to your left and turn right up the gravel track marked by blue and yellow arrows. Cross a cattle grid and continue along the track. Go downhill and over a bridge. Continue along the

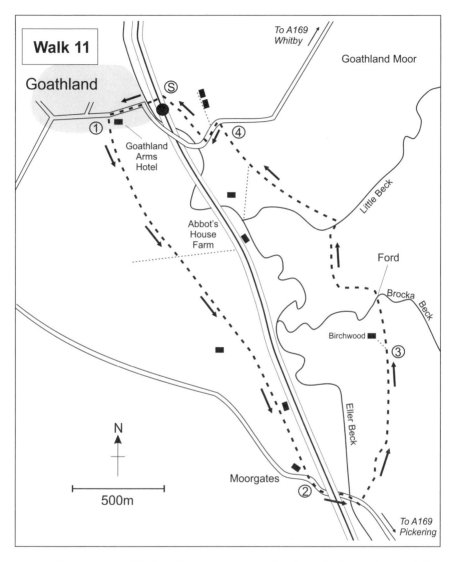

Walk 11

Goathland

To A169
Whitby

Goathland Moor

Goathland Arms Hotel

Little Beck

Abbot's House Farm

Ford

Brocka Beck

Birchwood

Eller Beck

Moorgates

To A169
Pickering

N

500m

road, now metalled or have a rest on the bench for a view of the railway.

There are good views of the North Yorkshire Moors Railway for the rest of the walk.

4. When you reach the road (busy!), turn left and walk downhill along the verge avoiding the sheep. Just before the right-hand bend, immediately before the 40mph sign, carefully cross the road and walk down the footpath to the right marked as a permissive bridleway.

Pass below some houses to your right and look out for a bench on your left, which marks the start of a grassy track following a wall steeply down hill. Follow this track until you reach the railway at the bottom.

Turn left through the white metal gate (£2 penalty for not shutting this gate!) and down 7 easy steps to return to the station.

Goathland Station has not only represented Aidensfield station, but was also transformed into Hogsmeade station in the first Harry Potter film, "Harry Potter and the Philosopher's Stone". If you look carefully you can just recognise it in the film, and many of the countryside rail scenes were filmed on this stretch of the North Yorkshire Moors Railway

In the area:

Trailways Cycle Hire at Hawsker near Whitby offers cycles for all the family as well as baby trailers and child seats. Ideal for exploring the coastal cycle trail. (www.trailways.info 01907 820207)

The National Railway Museum, York (01904 621261 www.nrm.org.uk) is the world's largest railway museum. Over three hundred years of world railway history are shown including Stephenson's Rocket, the Mallard, Japanese Bullet trains and Queen Victoria's favourite carriage. Excellent exhibitions and demonstrations, café, play area and miniature railway. You can easily spend a whole day here!

Walk 12: The Murk Esk, Grosmont

Allow: *2 hours (not including train ride)*

This is a one-way walk along the pretty Murk Esk River between Goathland and Grosmont. Both ends of the walk are reachable by the North Yorkshire Moors Railway and this makes a nice day out including the train-ride. The path follows the old Whitby to Pickering railway and is an easy gravel track, suitable for wheelchairs along most of its length.

The route can be done in either direction, though walking from Grosmont to Goathland involves a long uphill slog at the end, so we're recommending starting in Goathland. There are facilities in the villages at either end of the walk, and there is a pub and small shop in Beck Hole.

Make sure you allow enough time to get the last train back!!

Map: Ordnance Survey 1:25000 Explorer OL27 – grid reference 836013

Distance: 3½ miles (5.6km)

Getting there:
By train: Take the North Yorkshire Moors Railway to Goathland.
By car: From the A169 Pickering to Whitby road, turn off to Grosmont in the village of Sleights. Park in Grosmont and take the North York Moors Railway one stop to Goathland. (Or park in Goathland as for Walk 11 and return on the train after your walk).

From Goathland Station (also known as Hogwarts Station!) cross over the bridge and follow the road into the village. Pass the Goathland Arms Hotel and Aidensfield Garage. Ignore the first road on your right (toilets down this road) and continue past a row of shops on the left and houses on the right. Take the second road on the right to Darnholm and Beck Hole.

1. When you reach a footpath on your left, go through the gate to join the track signposted "Rail Trail Beck Hole". (If you get to a cross-roads you've gone too far!)

You can avoid the road through the village, but it involves lifting over 3 kissing gates. Take the footpath on the right-hand side just before the 40 mph sign. Walk past several houses to join a road, lifting over a kissing gate. Cross road, turn left and immediately right, lifting over a 2nd kissing gate marked by a sign for the "Grosmont Rail Trail". At the end of the path, lift over a 3rd kissing gate, cross the road and go through the gate immediately opposite to continue along the route described below.

Walk downhill through woodland with a small stream on your left. This is bumpy to start with but the track does smooth out. Come out of the woodland, through a small gate and past a house on your right, "Incline Cottage". Please respect their property as the footpath goes straight through their garden!

2. At the junction just past the house, go straight ahead. (Turn right here if you want to visit the pub and stream in Beck Hole!)

You are now walking along the route of the old Whitby to Pickering Railway. This opened in 1836 and was built by George Stevenson as a horse-drawn tramway. The railway was bought in 1845 by George Hudson, the "Railway King", and improved to take steam locomotives. It was in regular use until its closure in 1865 following the opening of the new railway between Goathland and Grosmont (now the North Yorkshire Moors Railway). The rails were left in place and the railway was re-opened between 1908-1914 as an autocar service, which ran during the summer from Whitby to Beck Hole. A sign on your left marks the site of the former Beck Hole railway station on this line.

Walk along the track looking out for evidence of the old railway and wild berries in late summer! There are benches along the route, with carvings depicting the horse-drawn carriages of days gone by.

Bridge over the Murk Esk

3. Ignore the Rail Trail footpath sign to your right (steps!) and instead carry on straight ahead. Cross the river by the old railway bridge and continue through pretty woodland along the river bank.

   Cross back over the river by a wooden footbridge and turn left following the wheelchair sign.

   After a couple of hundred metres, you can get down to the river side for picnics and paddling.

   Go through a gate, leaving the woodland and continue past open fields. Look out for a glimpse of trains as they go through the woods up to your right. Keep going along the track, through a gate to walk along with the river on your right. Pass a house on your right and continue along the track.

4. Go through a gate, past a row of terraced houses on your right, and continue along the track, now right next to the North Yorkshire Moors Railway.

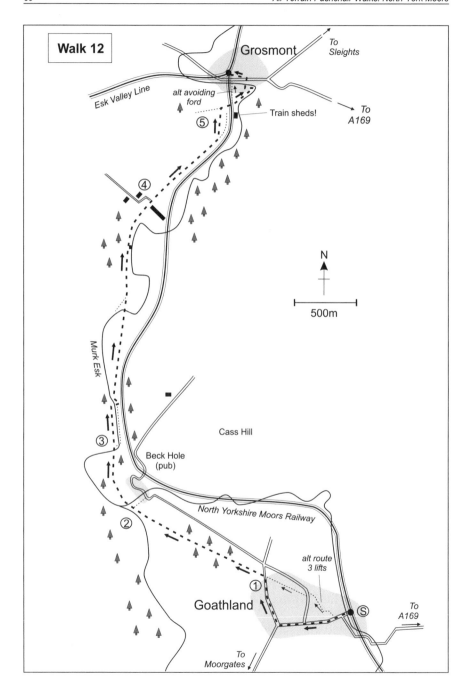

Walk 12

Grosmont

To Sleights

Esk Valley Line

alt avoiding ford

Train sheds!

To A169

⑤

④

N

500m

Murk Esk

Cass Hill

③

Beck Hole (pub)

②

North Yorkshire Moors Railway

alt route 3 lifts

①

Goathland

Ⓢ

To A169

To Moorgates

You'll go past old engines, signals and engine sheds – ideal for the steam train enthusiast!

5. When you get to a metal gate marked "Private Road", follow the footpath sign to the left and go through a long kissing gate, obviously designed specifically for ATPs! Push up the hill and up five easy, deep steps.

Down to your right is the engine shed viewing area where you can watch the trains being worked on.

At the top of the hill, go through the gate, have a rest on the bench and take in the view over Grosmont, and turn right to head down the hill towards the village.

At the next junction turn left through the kissing gate (Rail Trail) with the church on your right. Go along a narrow path, over a bridge and to Grosmont Station to get the train back!

For the more adventurous, instead of turning left continue straight ahead following the sign with a picture of a ruined building. Go down the hill with the church on your left until you reach the river. Turn left and over the cobbled ford. Go up the road opposite until you reach the main road opposite the Station Hotel. Turn left to get to the station. N.B. This part of the route is NOT advisable in wet weather as the ford is only passable in low water.

In the area:

The North Yorkshire Moors Railway runs from Pickering to Grosmont following the line of Stevenson's Whitby to Pickering railway. With 18 miles of preserved steam railway running through spectacular scenery, you can enjoy a day out on a steam train in the heart of the moors. Trains run throughout the year. Special events may need pre-booking (www.northyorkshiremoorsrailway.com).

Wild West Maize Maze, between Pickering and Thornton-le-Dale (01751 474354) is fun for all the family with a wagon-shaped maze, tepee, maze puzzle trail and picnic and play areas. Open 9.30-6pm, 7days a week, weather permitting.

Walk 13: Falling Foss and the Hermitage

Allow: *30 minutes or 1 hour*

A lovely walk through oak and ash woodland that takes you to both an 18th-century folly and an impressive waterfall. Falling Foss is the point at which May Beck flows over a 30ft (9m) precipice into Little Beck and this waterfall is most spectacular after heavy rain. Just a few minutes from the waterfall there is a shallow section of river next to an old stone bridge where the children can play in the water. This is also a great spot for a picnic.

Keep a look out for local wildlife because the woods surrounding May Beck and Little Beck are home to roe deer, foxes, badgers and the rare water vole. There are also an abundance of birds (including the Nightjar, wagtails and dippers), insects and the occasional reptile (adders and slow worms).

The short route misses out the folly and takes you down into the wooded valley bottom to the waterfall and picnic spot.

Map: Ordnance Survey 1:25000 Explorer OL27 – grid reference 888035

Distance: 0.5 or 1¼ miles (0.8 or 2km)

Getting there: Take the road signposted to Falling Foss from the B1416 between Ruswarp and Sneaton Corner. Park in the car park at the end of this road. There are picnic tables next to the car park.

Leave the car park via the entrance and go through the gap between the small stone wall and pillar straight ahead. Go down a few stone steps and onto a woodland path.

1. You will soon see a signpost ahead. To do the complete walk continue straight ahead towards Littlebeck (red posts mark this route). To do the short walk turn left in the direction of Falling Foss and follow the directions from **** on page 64.

The Hermitage

At the next signpost, which is alongside a few steps, turn left following the coast to coast route (red post with a white arrow).

2. Shortly you will see a large boulder ahead with 'The Hermitage' carved into it. This large sandstone folly has been carved out to make a resting place for weary travellers. This is the turning point of the walk and there is a great viewpoint here looking out over the wooded valley and Sleights Moor

The Hermitage is a folly that was carved out in 1760 by an unemployed seaman on the instructions of a local schoolmaster, George Chubb. Climb to the top of this huge hollowed out boulder and you will find two 'wishing chairs' carved out of rocks. It is said that if you sit in one chair and make a wish you must then sit in the second to make it come true.

Once you have admired The Hermitage and the view return along the same route until you reach the signpost directing you down a path on the right to Falling Foss.

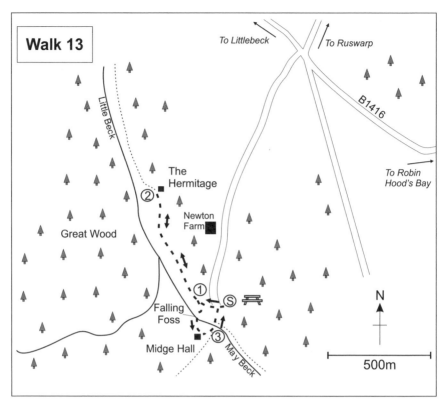

****Follow the narrow track down through the woods taking care for tree roots in the path. Be very careful with small children as there is a very steep drop to the right.

Go down a small number of steps and to your right you will be able to see the impressive waterfall, Falling Foss.

Continue along the path passing a derelict house on your right and cross a small footbridge. There is a lovely picnic spot next to the stream (May Beck) on your left and the water is usually shallow enough to paddle here in the summer months.

The derelict house is called Midge Hall and was built by Sir James Wilson for his gamekeeper and later became a museum.

3. Walk up the short steep slope, turn left and cross over the stone bridge. Continue up this broad gravel track up the hill and back to the car park.

In the area:

Ruswarp Pleasure Boats (www. ruswarp-pleasure-boats.co.uk) offer traditional rowing boats and canoes for you to explore the beautiful River Esk. Open March to October, 9am - 6pm.

Doodlepots, Whitby (01947 82582), is a creative studio where you can paint your own pottery from a selection of available pieces and you can even do your baby's hand and footprints. The studio glazes and fires your work ready for collection or to be posted to you. You pay for each piece plus a fixed fee per painter. Refreshments available. Open Monday – Saturday 10am-5pm.

Walk 14: Staindale Lake and the Bridestones, Dalby Forest

Allow: 2 hours

High and Low Staindale are situated in the heart of Dalby Forest, a Forestry Commission park. The name is derived from the Viking words meaning 'stony valley' and probably relates to the rocky ravines and the Bridestones rock formations. Staindale Lake was created relatively recently as a haven for ducks and geese. This is a great place to see a range of waterfowl including tufted ducks, goldeneye, and heron as well as many woodland birds.

The Bridestones are a group of Jurassic siliceous sandstone boulders that have been eroded into strange shapes by the wind and water over a period of 60,000 years. These amazing stone formations are situated in a nature reserve with SSSI status. There are three species of heather on the moorland surrounding the stones and the ancient oak woodlands adjoining the moors are thought to date back to the last Ice Age

The path around the Bridestones is cobbled and so is not recommended for very young babies. If you don't want to do the full walk then you can simply do a short walk (30 minutes) around the lake. This short route follows an accessible trail and so is very easy going.

Map: Ordnance Survey 1:25000 Explorer OL27 – grid reference 883904

Distance: 2¾ miles (4.4km)

Getting there: Park in the High Staindale car park on the Dalby Forest Drive. There is a toll to enter the forest but all parking is free.

Walk to the far end of the car park and follow the Staindale Lake Trail. Go straight ahead so that the lake is on your left, do not turn left over the footbridge. Stay on this path until you reach the far end of the lake. There are several picnic tables and benches along the banks of the lake.

**** To do the **short lake walk** simply follow the footpath around the lake instead of turning onto the road. The footpath will take you back to the car park.

1. At the far end of the lake you will come to the road, turn left and walk past Low Staindale car park and a toilet block with baby changing facilities.

Low Bridestones

Shortly after the toilets turn right into a car park and onto the Bridestones Trail. Follow the path into the woodland, don't go through a kissing gate on your left.

2. Turn left at the fork in the path and follow this track as it takes you gradually uphill to the Bridestones.

There are fantastic panoramic views from the Bridestones and the area is covered in bilberries which make a lovely snack on route in late August and September.

Stay on the cobbled path as it takes you past the Low Bridestones.

Ahead of you on the left you will be able to see a further set of stones, the High Bridestones.

3. At the next junction in the path turn left down the hill towards

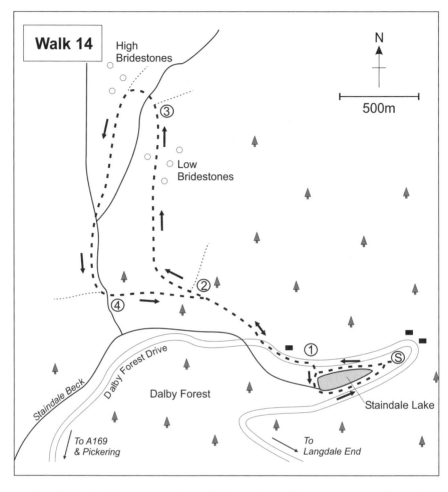

the High Bridestones, don't follow the yellow arrow to the right. This takes you down a bumpy path, across a small easily negotiated stream and then back up the hill.

Follow the path as it bears round to the left leaving the stones behind you. The path now becomes a dirt track and can be narrow in places. Go down a steep cobbled downhill section where it is advisable to use a pram leash for safety.

4. Follow the path as it takes you over two footbridges to a kissing gate. It may be possible to squeeze the pushchair through the kissing gate but we found it easier to lift it over the fence to the side.

Follow the track along with Staindale Beck on your right and eventually this will lead you to a kissing gate alongside a gate. The gate is usually open but if locked lift the pushchair over. Turn right and follow the path back down to the car park.

Turn left onto the road and walk past the toilet block to the lake. Turn right and follow the lakeside trail with the lake on your left. This path will lead you all the way back to the High Staindale car park.

In the area:

The Purple Mountain Bike Hire (www.purplemountain.co.uk), 01751 417856 in Dalby Forest offers bikes for all family members including kiddie trailers and child seats. You can even hire a tandem and there is a café at the hire centre.

Playdale Farm Park, Cayton (www. playdalefarmpark.co.uk) offers a fun day out where you can walk amongst the farm animals and play in the large indoor play area with ball pool, toddler area, tractor zone and adventure trail! There is also an outdoor play area with climbing frame and sandpit complete with diggers. Café, shop and toilets with baby changing facilities. Open March to September from 10am.

Walk 15: Whisperdales

Allow: 2 hours 30 minutes

This is a challenging walk through Broxa Forest and the peaceful valleys of Whisperdales and Highdales. These valleys are truly remote, with no road up Whisperdales and some very large fords at the entrance to Highdales. There are no wires to obscure the views as the houses at the end of the valley have their own generators to provide electricity. There is also no mobile phone signal, so you're in for a truly peaceful time!

Most of the walk is on forestry tracks and farm tracks across fields, and can get very muddy in wet weather. There is a VERY tough uphill section from Highdales to return to Broxa Forest, which is only for the very fit and those experienced in off-roading with a pushchair. However, the walk can be made easier by a simple there-and-back route down Whisperdales.

The fords may become impassable in very wet conditions (the road sometimes looks like a river!).

Map: Ordnance Survey 1:25000 Explorer OL27 – grid reference 965944

Distance: 4½ miles (7.2km)

Getting there: From the A171 between Whitby and Scarborough, turn off towards Harwood Dale. Park in the North Riding Forestry Commission car park on Reisty Hill on the south side of the road.

Follow the broad forest track leading from the car park signposted public bridleway. Continue down this track ignoring a right turn beyond a barrier, and head round the track to the left and down hill into Whisperdales.

1. At the bottom of the hill, pass Whisperdales Farm keeping the house on your right. Go straight ahead through a small gate next to the bridlepath sign. Follow this track, which is rutted and

Lowdales Ford!

muddy in wet weather, through the fields beside a small stream, Whisperdales Beck.

Where the track forks just beyond a small stream, take the right-hand fork heading towards a white arrow on a wooden post.

Go through a second gate and over a small stream and continue along the track with the stream on your right.

There are nice spots for a picnic beside the stream, but this is not access land so respect the landowner's property.

Go through a third gate and continue along the track heading towards a red roofed house at the bottom of the valley.

Pass through a fourth gate and continue along the track beside a hedge, towards the house.

Go past the house until you get to a ford. Either cross the ford or go

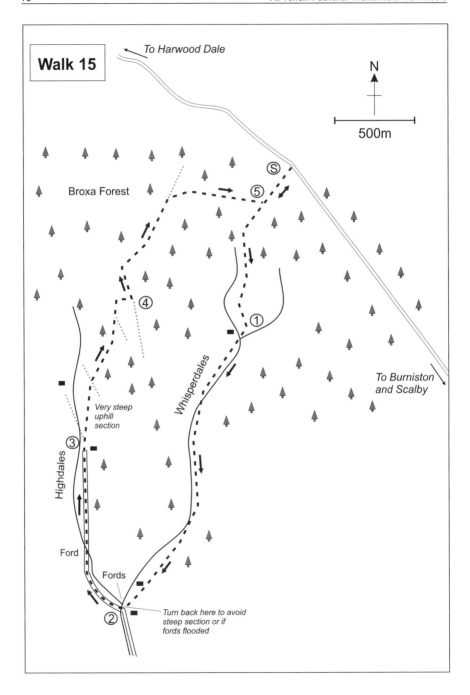

Walk 15

To Harwood Dale

N

500m

Broxa Forest

To Burniston
and Scalby

Whisperdales

Highdales

Very steep
uphill
section

Ford

Fords

Turn back here to avoid
steep section or if
fords flooded

over the footbridge and lift over the stile at the far end of the bridge. Pass a house on the left and go through the second and third fords (or over their corresponding bridges) to join the road.

At time of writing the third ford, Lowdales ford, had turned the road into a river which disappeared off round the corner.... This is quite a common occurrence and this must be one of the longest fords in Britain! If the fords are impassable or you want to avoid a steep and awkward uphill climb, turn back here and retrace your route through Whisperdales.

2. Turn right and walk along the road up the hill into Highdales, ignoring footpaths to the left and right. Cross a fourth ford.

At the end of the road, ignore a footpath over a fence to your right and go through the gate to continue along a track keeping the house on your right.

3. Just before the second gate, leave the track to take a steep muddy path uphill signposted public bridleway.

This is the hardest part of the walk and is a very tough uphill push in wet weather.

Continue uphill (it may be easier to pull!) until you reach a large skewed cross-roads where you continue straight ahead up the path. Keep going up the hill into the plantation. Ignore minor tracks to the right but keep going until the track levels out and bends round to the right at the edge of a freshly cleared area of forest.

Follow the track to a T-junction with a broad gravel forest track – easy going at last!

4. Turn left onto the forest track to head back into the trees. Ignore a junction to the left and grassy tracks to the right, and follow the main track as it curves round to the left.

Turn right along a very obvious gravelled track and continue to a white barrier ignoring minor grassy tracks to the left and right.

5. Go around the barrier and turn left to walk back to the car park and your car.

In the area:

Scarborough Sea Life Centre (www.sealifeeurope.com) offers insight into a magical marine world where you can see thousands of sea creatures from around the globe. Go underwater to view the marine life, without getting wet, visit the seals or have a drink in the café while the kids enjoy themselves in the soft play area. Open all year from 10am.

Kinderland in Scarborough's North Bay (www.kinderland.co.uk) offers a fun day out in a 4.5 acres of landscaped grounds. The site offers traditional play structures and activities, all easily accessible for those with prams (or ATPs!). There are too many activities to list here but you only pay once. Open March – September.

Walk 16: Forge Valley and Ayton Castle, West Ayton

Allow: 1 hour or 2 hours

This is a beautiful walk along the banks of the River Derwent at the base of the deep ravine of Forge Valley. The valley was formed by glacial melt-waters at the end of the last ice age. The name of the valley dates back to the 14th century when the monks of Rievaulx worked iron forges here. The woods surrounding the River Derwent were coppiced to produce charcoal to power these ironstone smelting forges. This is now one the areas richest deciduous woodlands which supports a broad range of animal and plant life. So keep your eyes open as there is plenty to see in this popular beauty spot.

There are several options for this walk depending on how energetic and daring you feel! The easiest option is a simple 'there-and-back' walk along the boardwalk on the banks of the River Derwent. If you want to go a little further and can handle a stile, then do a there-and-back to the castle. The full circular walk is for the more adventurous. The path through the woodland is narrow and there are some very awkward strenuous sections to negotiate. There is also a steep stepped downhill section, which would be best approached with two people.

Map: Ordnance Survey 1:25000 Explorer OL27 – grid reference 984871

Distance: 1½ or 3 or 4 miles (2.4 or 4.8 or 6.4km)

Getting there: Park in Old Man's Mouth car park on the Forge Valley road. There are picnic tables and a footbridge across the river next to the car park.

Cross the river at the footbridge and turn left so you are walking along the boardwalk with the river on your left.

The boardwalk takes you three-quarters of a mile towards West

Ayton, following the river bank all the way. At the end of this path you will come to a stile. If you want to do the easy walk and don't want to see the castle then turn back now.

1. To continue the walk, lift the pushchair over the stile and follow the path across the meadow.

   Keep to the right edge of the meadow and eventually turn right up a track to a gateway. Go through the gateway and follow the path around the field. Ayton Castle will soon come into view. If you don't want

Forge Valley boardwalk

to do the full circular walk, turn back now.

It is thought that a castle was originally built on this site by Gilbert, first lord of Ayton, before his death in 1350. The castle and estates were passed down to his granddaughter who married Sir Ralph de Eure. Sir Ralph added a three storey stone tower in the 14th century. Occupation of the castle ended in the 17th century and after a long list of owners it finally became the property of Scarborough Council in 1930.

Follow the path as it takes you to the left of the castle and towards a locked gate with a narrow kissing gate alongside. Lift the push-

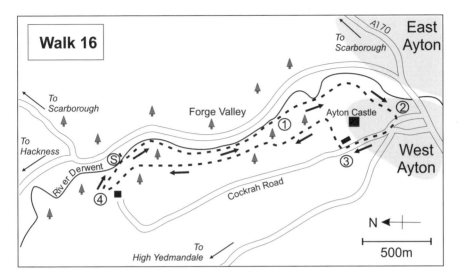

chair over this and follow the road ahead past some houses (Castle Rise).

2. Turn right at the end of Castle Rise and at the end of this road (Yedmandale Road) turn right again onto a no-through road (Cockrah Road).

3. Walk up the road and just past West Ayton Caravan Club Site turn down a public footpath on the right. Go through the gates and along the broad track until you reach the end of the field where you turn left away from the caravan park.

The path takes you along the edge of the field with the gorge on your right. At the end of this field you must turn right down a narrow track into the woodland.

This is a narrow path and there are a few tricky sections and some tree roots to negotiate.

4. Follow the path for three-quarters of a mile (approximately 30 minutes) and soon after it heads downhill turn right onto a narrow stepped path that down into the gorge.

This is a difficult section and requires two people as some lifting may be required.

The path takes you back down to the boardwalk alongside the River Derwent. Turn right and then left to cross the river at the footbridge and return to the car park.

In the area:

Betton Farm, in East Ayton (www.bettonfarm.co.uk), is a children's animal farm and play centre where you can explore the farm and meet the animals before playing on the toy tractors and adventure playground. For adults there is a tea room, farm shop and bakery. Open all year 10am-5pm.

Atlantis, in Scarborough's North Bay , is a heated outdoor waterpark and offers plenty of excitement for all the family. Wallow in the bubbles, visit pirate's cove or brave the river rapids before having refreshments in the Galley café. Open end May to early September, 10am-6pm (www.discoveryorkshirecoast.com).

Walk 17: Common Cliff, Ravenscar

Allow: 1 hour 30 minutes

This is a lovely walk along a rugged coast path with fantastic views. The path takes you past an old radar station and then onto the dismantled Scarborough to Whitby railway. The paths are excellent and easy along the majority of the route and there is just one low stile to negotiate.

The settlement at Ravenscar dates back to Roman times but is now famous for being the town that never was. A group of business men led by John Septimus Bland decided to turn the area into a new holi-day resort to rival Scarborough and Whitby. The success of the Scarborough to Whitby railway meant that investors were plenty and work soon began. The drainage system and roads were laid out and a small number off houses and shops built. However, the absence of a sandy beach and instability of the cliffs meant there was a lack of interest from the public. The developers went bankrupt and the project was abandoned in 1913.

Ravenscar also has connections with Royalty as mad King George III was treated in the Raven Hall Hotel (then named Peak House) by the Rev. Dr. Francis Willis for his bouts of insanity. Treatment consisted of bleeding with leeches, constraint and deluging in baths of water!

Map: Ordnance Survey 1:25000 Explorer OL27 – grid reference 985012

Distance: 2½ miles (4km)

Getting there: Park in the square next to the old Ravenscar railway station on Station Road, Ravenscar. There is a very friendly tea shop next to the green (Ravenscar Tea Rooms) which sells great hot and cold food, has a baby seat and toilets (Open Easter till the end of September except Wednesdays). There are also benches next to the old station. There is a National Trust Coastal Centre and toilets in the village of Ravenscar.

Ravenscar cliffs

Walk over the road and down the stony path towards the coast. Turn right onto the Cleveland way.

This path follows the unprotected cliff edge so take care especially with walking children. There are several benches along this route.

The grassy path takes you past the derelict Ravenscar Radar Station and coastguard lookout tower.

Ravenscar Radar Station was used in World War 2 and was one of a series of stations that made up the Coastal Defence Chain Home Low. The radar stations were used to detect invading German ships and aircraft. Ravenscar was a short range station which allowed detection of planes flying close to the sea. This meant that the Germans were unable to fly low to avoid detection.

There is a short cut shortly after the radar station along a National Trust permitted path on your right. This short cut takes you to the dismantled railway line and reduces the route considerably. However it still involves lifting the pushchair over a stile.

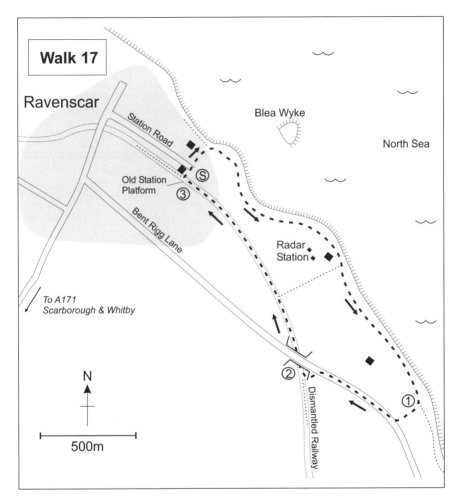

1. Eventually, turn right over a stile signposted as a footpath. The path takes you across a field to a gateway onto a very quiet country lane.

2. Turn right onto the road and follow it until you see a path down to your left. This path is just before you cross a bridge over the railway. Go down the path and turn right onto the old railway path and go under a bridge.

   You will be able to see Beacon Windmill over to your left.

3. Follow the track until you come to a gate with the old Ravenscar station platform straight ahead. Go through the gate and turn right down a path back to the parking area and tea rooms.

The Scarborough to Whitby railway (opened in 1885) was closed in 1965 by Dr Beeching. It is now a well maintained walking and cycling trail.

In the area:

Staintondale Shirehorse Farm (www.shirehorsefarm.co.uk), between Scarborough and Whitby, is offers live horse shows, including cowboy tricks, and supervised hands-on experience for children with Shetland ponies. You can also walk round some of the coastal scenery to look at the views, hedgerows and pond. Picnic and play areas, cafe and souvenir shop. Open end May to September, Sunday, Tuesday, Wednesday and Friday.

Scarborough Castle (www.english-heritage.org.uk) dominates the town standing high on the headland separating North and South Bays. The site has been a defence for 2500 years and the present remains date from the 12th to 14th centuries. The headland has magnificent views up and down the coast and it is easy to imagine why this site was chosen as the town's defence. Open all year.

Walk 18: Fyling Hall to Ramsdale Mill, Fylingthorpe

Allow: 1 hour 30 minutes

This is a pleasant walk up a picturesque wooded valley to Ramsdale Mill, one of two old watermills in the area (now a private house). The mill was obviously built to take advantage of the natural power of the water as it heads down the steep valley and the waterwheel is still in place.

The walk is long a good track for its entire length, which does provide access to the mill, so watch out for the odd car. Facilities in Fylingthorpe village.

Map: Ordnance Survey 1:25000 Explorer OL27 – grid reference 934045

Distance: 2 miles (3.2km)

Getting there: From the A171 turn off to Fylingthorpe and Robin Hood's Bay. Take the first turning to Fyling Hall and park just before the first green grit bin on the left (space for two cars).

Continue on foot down the road and at the junction turn right to walk through the gateposts to Fyling Hall School.

Fyling Hall, now an independent school, is a fine example of a Georgian country house. It was built in 1819 by Squire John Warren Barry, a Whitby ship owner who was also known for building a pig sty near Robin Hood's Bay in the form of a Grecian Temple! Fyling Hall has been a school since 1923.

1. Opposite the school, turn right up a public bridle path and follow it up hill. Watch out for vehicles on this track as it is the access road to the mill and adjacent houses.

   Continue along the track ignoring a rough track off to the right and carry on walking high up along the valley side.

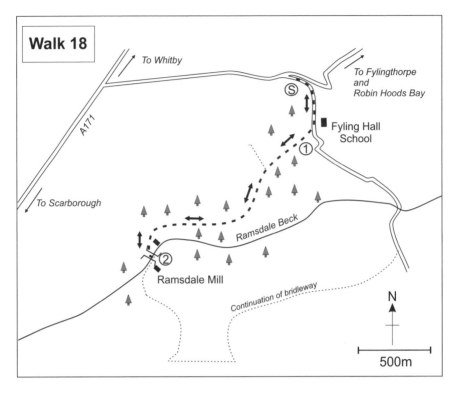

There are lovely views back to Robin Hood's Bay nestling amongst the cliffs and down to the rocky headlands north of Ravenscar.

Continue back into woodland and cross two small streams as the track bends round to the right.

2. Carry on until you get to the mill, which is the end of our walk. Return along the route you came.

The water mill, one of two in the area, takes advantage of the power of Ramsdale Beck as it crashed down the steep valley to the sea. There has been a mill on this site since at least the 17th century, when it was in the possession of Whitby Abbey. The present building dates from 1858.

Ramsdale Mill

In the area:

Robin Hood's Bay **Old Coastguard Station visitor centre** (www.nationaltrust.org.uk) has exhibitions on fossils, dinosaur footprints, a marine aquarium, local sea life and information of what you can find on the beaches and in the cliffs. Open weekends all year and weekdays (except Monday) June – September.

Beacon Farm in Sneaton (www.beacon-farm.co.uk) produces traditional ice cream in many flavours from the milk and cream from Yorkshire cows. The tea room offers stunning views of Whitby Abbey and the Yorkshire Coast. There is a children's play area with free bouncy castle. Open all year except January, 10am – 5pm. Weekends only in winter.

Walk 19: Whitby Abbey to Saltwick Nab

Allow: 1 hour 30 minutes

Whitby is an ancient seaport and fishing town built where the River Esk reaches the North Sea. It is built on two steep cliffs overlooking the harbour and has attractive winding streets and many old buildings. The explorer, Captain James Cook first sailed from Whitby, and his ships the Endeavour and Resolution were built in here. The town is also famous for jet, a semi-precious stone and form of fossilised wood, which is found along this coast. It has been used in jewellery for several thousand years and was made popular in the 19th century by Queen Victoria. Finally, Whitby is notorious for its role in Bram Stoker's novel Dracula. The vampire landed in Britain here aboard a crewless ship, with its dead captain lashed to the helm. When the ship crash landed, Dracula came ashore in the form of a large dog, and his first British victim was bitten here!

This walk takes you along part of the coastal path with its spectacular views and cliffs. You return through the centre of town and up the narrow and steep streets before finally climbing up east cliff next to the famous 199 steps. Though partly a town walk, this route is very strenuous with some extremely steep inclines!

Map: Ordnance Survey 1:25000 Explorer OL27 – grid reference 903110

Distance: 3 miles (4.8km)

Getting there: In Whitby, follow the brown signs to Whitby Abbey. Park in the Abbey car park (fee).

From the car park entrance, turn left along the road with the Abbey on your left. Continue along the road until you reach a farm.

The Abbey is dedicated to St Hilda and was a Benedictine monastery founded in 657 AD by the Saxon King of Northumbria.

Whitby Abbey

Both monks and nuns resided here and it was also home to the famous Saxon poet, Caedmon. It was attacked by Vikings in the 9th century and was abandoned for 200 years. Refounded in 1078, the monastery survived until Henry VIII's dissolution of the monasteries when it was finally destroyed in 1540. It has remained a prominent landmark ever since.

1. Cross the road (going down the steep grassy verge!) and turn right down a farm track marked with a yellow arrow on a wooden post, signposted "Cleveland Way, Robin Hood's Bay". Pass the house to the right and go through a gate. Continue along the track with the radio transmitter and coastguard lookout on your left. Go through a big wooden kissing gate and turn right to walk along the coast path.

As you walk towards the first headland you can see the remains of a shipwreck in the bay below you, when the tide is out.

Continue along the path, avoiding a flight of steps to their right. Continue to the sea stacks of Saltwick Nab.

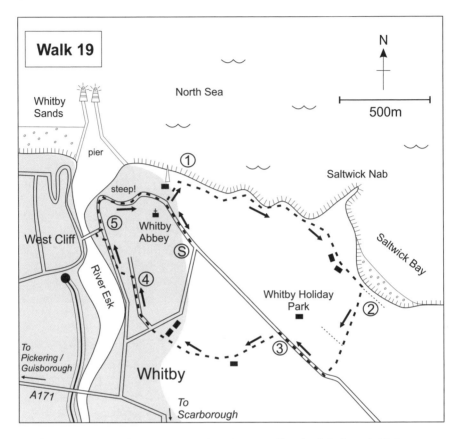

Once the site of an alum works, the headland of Saltwick Nab is more renowned for its shipwrecks, the most famous of which was the Rohilla, a hospital ship which ran aground here in a storm during a coastal blackout in 1914. She was broken up by the waves and 84 of the 229 crew died, despite being only a few hundred metres from the shore.

Follow the path into the holiday park. When you come to a junction, turn left and walk past the playground towards the holiday park where, as well as buying a caravan, you could stop in the pub or café.

2. Continue down the holiday park driveway, watching out for traf-

fic. When you reach the road, turn right and walk along the road for about 150m.

3. Cross over and turn left down a public footpath, which is rough. Lift over the kissing gate (awkward and high) and continue through the farmyard.

If you don't want to lift over the gate, the road takes you right back to the Abbey.

Continue down the farm track. When the road bends to the right past some houses, take the narrow, walled path to the left of the houses heading straight ahead. Look out for nettles at pushchair height!

When you reach the road, cross over and continue straight over down the road marked "except for access". Keep following the road until a fork.

4. At the fork, head down the path with a central railing and a "no bikes" sign. This leads to a steep cobbled path to the harbour. At the bottom of the hill, cross the road and turn right to walk along the harbour.

Look out for the man on roller skates adorning a building on your right! These are the Merchant Seaman's hospital houses founded 1675. (The roller skates are actually scrolls...)

Continue until you come to the end of a car park on your left. Turn left down the pedestrian Grape Lane and past the Captain Cook Memorial Museum on your left, built in 1688.

This is the house where Captain James Cook lived from 1746 during his initial time as an apprentice in Whitby. Cook (1728-1779) was a Whitby-based explorer, navigator and cartographer, famous for his exploration of the South Pacific on the ships Endeavour and Resolution. His achievements include the discovery of the east coast of Australia, Hawaii and the mapping of New Zealand. The transit of Venus across the face of the sun, from which the distance between the sun and the earth can be measured, was first recorded in 1769 during his first Pacific voyage as captain of the Endeavour. He died in 1779 on his third voyage (1776-1780), in command of the Resolution. After an initial friendly welcome in Hawaii, Cook was killed by natives when his ship was forced to return there during bad weather and relationships soured.

The lane brings you to the bridge over the River Esk. Over the bridge is the harbour, tourist information centre, boat cruises, the Grand Turk boat and the Bark Endeavour; a small scale replica of Captain Cook's famous ship.

When you've done in the centre of town, head right from the end of Grape Lane to walk back up to the Abbey.

5. Turn left at the first junction following the signs to the Abbey. Follow the road round to the right and up the VERY steep hill!!!

The famous 199 steps are to the left of the road, which you could try for a challenge. But if you lose count you have to go down to the bottom and start again... The steps lead to St Mary's church where the date of Easter was fixed by the Synod in 664. The churchyard is also the setting for the biting of Dracula's first British victim!

At the top of the hill you come to a metalled area and, if you're lucky, an ice cream van.

For a well-earned rest, pause here to look back at the view across to West Cliff where you can see the white arch of the whale jawbone, which is the start of Walk 20.

Follow the wall around to the right to meet the road by the farm you passed at the start of the walk. Continue along the road until you reach the Abbey car park and your car.

In the area:

Whitby Abbey (www.english-heritage.org.uk/whitbyabbey) located at the headland of East Cliff was a Benedictine monastery founded in 657 AD. Today, it is a series of impressive ruins high above the sea providing an ideal site for young explorers. Tea-room, toilets and disabled access.

Whitby Bark Endeavour (01723 364100), berthed in Whitby harbour is a 40% sized replica of Captain Cook's famous ship. Take a sailing on board and learn all about Cook and his expeditions while you travel up the coast to Sandsend.

Walk 20: West Cliff and Whitby Sands

Allow: 1 hour

This is an easy walk with a steep ascent at the end! It starts on West Cliff, high above the harbour with stunning views across to the Abbey and St Hilda's Church on the opposite side. There's even the chance for sandcastle building as you walk along the lovely Whitby Sands.

The going is very easy along metalled paths and sand so this walk is suitable for those with small babies. You can even opt out of the final climb by taking the cliff lift! The beach gets cut off at high tide so check tide times before you go.

Map: Ordnance Survey 1:25000 Explorer OL27 – grid reference 897114

Distance: 1¾ miles (2.8km)

Getting there: Park in the West Cliff car park in Whitby or along the roadside on North Terrace.

The walk begins at the pair of whale jaw bones at the end of North Terrace (above West Pier) so leave your car and make your way towards these.

Whitby was once a prosperous whaling town and it is documented that 2761 whales were landed here. When a whaling boat returned to harbour it would hang the whale jaw bones on the mast to let those waiting on land know that the trip had been successful. The jaw bones displayed at West Cliff today were presented to Whitby by King Thor of Norway in 1963 to commemorate the memory of these hard times.

Turn right in front of the whale bones and walk along the pavement until you come to a fork in the path. Take the left-hand fork and

follow the path as it gradually goes down the hill
and over some cobbles.

The path takes you back
to the road, so follow this
as it winds down the hill
towards the pier.

1. At the bottom of the
   road turn left and walk
   down the slipway to
   the beach passing the
   round beach shop on
   your left.

If you want to extend
your walk then you
could go to the
lighthouse at the end
of the pier before you
go down to the beach.

Walk along the beach
with the pier behind
you.

Whitby Sands and the pier lighthouses

On a clear day you will be able to see Sandsend straight ahead.

2. Leave the beach by walking up the first concrete slope that you
   see on your left. Walk along this raised walkway and past the
   beach huts. Turn left after you have passed a small building and
   follow the path as it zigzags up the hill.

Those who don't fancy the walk back up the hill can take the Cliff
Lift back up to North Terrace.

3. Turn left at the top of the hill back onto North Terrace and walk
   back to your car.

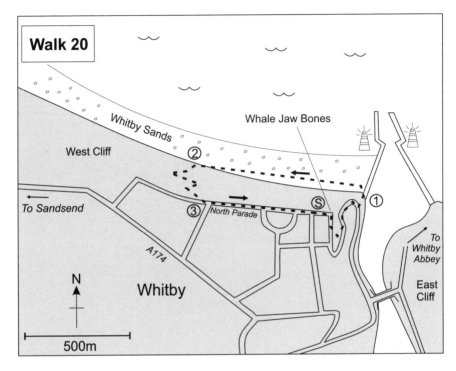

In the area:

Yellow Boats located in Whitby Harbour offer daily trips out into the bay. Trips last 25-30 minutes or you can take a longer trip up the coast to Staithes. Under 5's free (www.whitbycoastalcruises.co.uk).

Dracula Experience on Marine Parade, Whitby (01947 601923) offers life-like models with an animated ship, opening coffins and actors to give you a fright! Open all year, weekends only in winter.

Walk 21: Mulgrave Castle Woods, Sandsend

Allow: *2 hours*

A walk through beautiful broadleaved and conifer woodland alongside the pretty stream, East Row Beck. The walk takes you to the ruins of old Mulgrave Castle, a 13th-century stone enclosure fortress. Old Mulgrave Castle is said to have been built by a twelve foot giant named Wade, who was in fact a Viking chieftain. He was involved in the murder of King Ethelred and built the castle to protect himself from revenging friends of the king. Wade is said to be buried near Goldsborough (see Walk 22) where there are two gravestones half a mile apart, which mark the head and foot of the grave.

The estate is open on Saturday, Sunday and Wednesday throughout the year but is closed for the whole of May. Dogs are allowed.

Map: Ordnance Survey 1:25000 Explorer OL27 – grid reference 861124

Distance: 3¾ miles (6km)

Getting there: Park in East Row car park next to East Row Beck and the beach at Sandsend (fee payable).

Go through the gate at the far end of the car park into the Mulgrave Estate and follow the broad tarmac road into the woodland.

The stream to your left is East Row Beck.

The path takes you through a timber mill and continues into the woods. Pass a house on your right, go through a gateway and continue on the road straight ahead. Stay on this main path, ignoring turnings to the left and right.

There was said to be a fairy named Jeanie who lived deep in the heart of Mulgrave Woods. Jeanie was a happy and peaceful fairy but had a bad temper. When a curious young farmer's boy found her

Old Mulgrave Castle

hiding place she was so angry that she chased him out of the forest. The boy knew that fairies couldn't cross water and so headed for the closest stream. He was just crossing the stream when Jeanie caught up with him and although she couldn't cross she managed to strike his horses rear with her wand. The animal perished in the water but the farmer's boy escaped.

1. You will eventually come to a junction (1½ miles) with a right-hand turning down through a tunnel. Turn left here in the direction of the old castle.

   Continue straight ahead ignoring a second sign for the castle pointing to a stepped path on the right.

2. At the next crossroads turn right up the hill. Turn right again at a second crossroads and follow the track up to the castle. The track then passes to the right of the castle; it is possible to take a look inside by going up a small number of steps on your left.

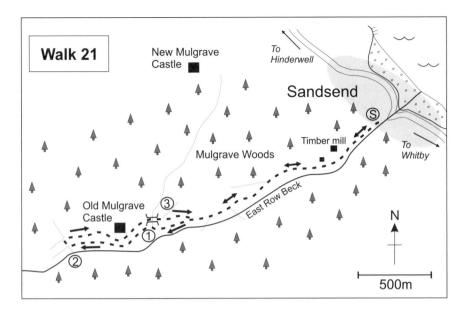

The castle was built in 1214 and has had a chequered history since that time. In the 14th century a square tower was added and in the 16th-century Elizabethan mullioned windows were put in. The castle has acted as a prison for captives of King John and as a centre for poaching and cattle raiding. The castle was besieged twice during the civil war and then blown up. It has been in the ownership of the Phipps family since the 18th century and in recent years has been repaired to its present state.

Return to the path and continue along with the castle on your left. This takes you away from the castle, over the tunnel you saw earlier.

3. Immediately after the tunnel the path forks. Take the right-hand fork down the hill, which takes you back onto the main track. Simply follow this track all the way back to the car.

In the area:

Sandsend Beach is a stunning sandy beach located 3 miles north of Whitby, ideal for paddling and building sandcastles. Sandsend village has a selection of facilities including cafés (the one in the car park has changing facilities and a potty!), toilets, pub and shop.

Whitby Wizard Hands-on Science (01947 810470) is a new interactive attraction located on West Cliff. The museum has a large collection of exciting hands-on exhibits in the region, suitable for both adults and children and you can try magical experiments for yourself! Open weekends and holidays all year, weekdays (except Monday) from Easter to September.

Walk 22: Kettleness to Goldsborough

Allow: *2 hours*

A great walk up the route of a dismantled railway and along farm lanes. There is plenty to see along the route including mines, coastal views, Roman remains and a giant's grave! There are a couple of stiles on the full circular walk. However, if you want to avoid these then simply do a 'there-and-back' walk along the old railway track. This track runs all the way to Runswick so if you have a couple of cars then you could park one at either end.

Kettleness was once a thriving alum mining centre and evidence of this time can clearly be seen at Kettleness Point. However, the village was devastated on the night of 17th December 1829 when the cliff collapsed and a large part of the village slipped down into the sea. No-one was hurt as the village had been evacuated and the mining was of such importance to the area that it was back in full swing within five years of the disaster. All that remains of the village now are a few cottages, a farm and the old Victorian railway station.

Map: Ordnance Survey 1:25000 Explorer OL27 – grid reference 830156

Distance: 4 miles (6.4km)

Getting there: Take the road (Goldsborough Lane) signposted to Kettleness from the A174 between Lythe and Hinderwell. Turn left in Goldsborough in the direction of Kettleness. Drive to the end of the road and park just before the farm. There is a bench here with fantastic coastal views.

Walk back up the road away from the coast towards the old Kettleness station which is now a scout hut. Turn right after the old station onto a broad track. Go through a gateway and continue on the track ahead.

This track is the route of the old Whitby to Middlesbrough railway line which was in service between 1883 and 1958. There is a bench here from which you can admire the great views up the coast. You will soon be able to see a lovely beach, Runswick Sands, down to your right. As you walk along this section of the track you will see a path on your left that goes through the field and up a small hill. There are disused mine shafts here.

1. Pass a carved bench which has images of the railway on it and is dated 1883 – 2001. Soon after this you will come to a further gateway (if you pass under a bridge then you have walked too far).

If you do not want to lift your pushchair over any stiles then you can continue walking along the disused railway track. Turn back at your leisure and return along the same route.

Turn right immediately before this gate into the grass field. Walk along the left-hand hedge until you see a path to your left that crosses over an old railway bridge.

Go over the bridge and lift the pushchair over the stile at the end.

Baaa!!

Go through the gateway ahead and into another field. Follow the left-hand edge of the field up to another gateway and stile. Lift the pushchair over the stile and continue straight ahead up to the farm house (don't turn left over another stile).

2. Go through the gate or over the stile just before the farm and continue straight ahead keeping the farm to your right. Go over or round the cattle grid and continue walking up the farm lane.

Continue along this farm lane passing over five more cattle grids (some of these have gateways to the side) and going past Brockrigg Farm on the way. Eventually the lane will bring you to a road (Goldsborough Lane).

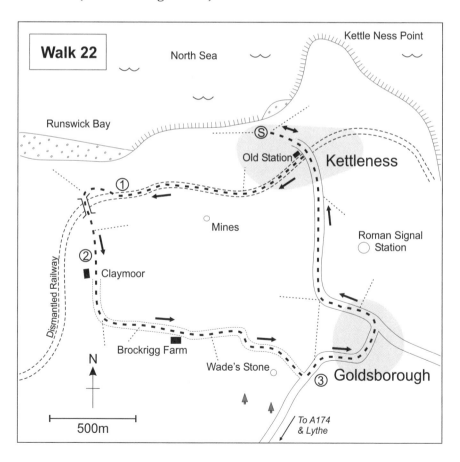

Just before you reach the road you will see a standing stone in the middle of the field on your right. This is Wade's Stone and is one of a pair of standing stones that are said to mark the head and feet of the giant Wade's grave. The second of the two stones is located next to the A174 at East Barnby. The stones are more than half a mile apart making Wade a very large giant indeed!

3. Turn left onto the road and follow it down into the village of Goldsborough.

There are great views down the coast from this road and you can also see the church in Lythe.

In the middle of Goldsborough take the road on the left in the direction of Kettleness.

If you want to stop for refreshments then continue to the right through the village of Goldsborough and you will find a pub (The Fox and Hounds) which is open at lunch times Wednesday to Sunday.

Follow the road all the way down the hill to Kettleness and find your car at the end.

To the right of this final stretch of road there lie the remains (earthworks only) of a 4th-century Roman signal station. Excavations of this site have unearthed remains that suggest that the signal station may have come to an abrupt end.

In the area:

Mungle Jungle in Redcar is an all-weather fun centre for kids under 10. Under-fives' play area, bouncy castle, slides, ball pool and much more. Cafe and toilets available 01642 483520. Open all year.

Saltburn Miniature Railway (01642 502863), is a 15-inch gauge railway from the seafront through to the lovely Valley Gardens, Italian Gardens, Tea Lawn and Woodland Centre. Open Easter to end-Sept & Bank Holidays, Sat & Sun, 1pm - 5pm. Events in the woodland centre throughout the year.

Walk 23: Scaling Dam

Allow: 1 hour 15 minutes

This is an easy there-and-back walk along Scaling Dam, which helps contain Scaling Reservoir, the largest body of water on the Moors. The reservoir is popular for watersports with sailing and fishing, so you can watch the boats on the water. Take care of fisherman casting flies though!

There is a pub with an adventure playground on the road opposite the dam and a sandwich van in the half-way car park, so there are plenty of eating opportunities, or you can take your own picnic to enjoy in the picnic site at the end of the walk.

Map: Ordnance Survey 1:25000 Explorer OL27 – grid reference 740125

Distance: 2½ miles (4km)

Getting there: From the A171 turn off at the Scaling Dam Watersports sign, past the Northumbrian Water sign and park in the car park on the right.

Walk through the car park and past the visitor centre to the dam.

Picnic tables and information board by the dam.

Head onto the dam and pass the white gate to its left. N.B. There are no protective fences on the steep-sided dam and the reservoir is deep, so keep children under strict control. Walk along the dam, looking out for water birds and watching the sailing boats.

1. At the end of the dam continue along the obvious broad, grassy track and follow a gravel path over the overflow channel to a car park.

Toilets, picnic tables and, if you're lucky, a food or ice-cream van can be found here.

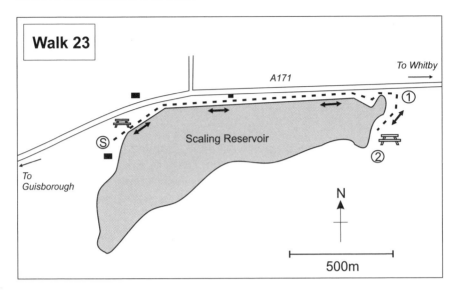

Continue along the gravel path following the lake shore to an information board and through a broad kissing gate. Cross the wooden footbridge and continue along the gravel path.

The reservoir is home to lots of wildlife including the green hair-streaked butterfly, Britain's only green-winged butterfly. This can be seen from late April-early June and its caterpillars feed on the local bilberries. Birds visiting the reservoir include lapwing, oystercatchers and mallards.

2. Keep going until you come to a picnic area at the water's edge. Here there are lovely views across the lake and information boards on the birds, butterflies and flora found by the lake.

There is a circular path around the lake but this is not on a defined footpath and is not suitable for pushchairs. The path is closed when the reservoir water is high.

Once you have picnicked to your heart's content, walk back the way you came across the dam to your car.

Scaling Reservoir

In the area:

Saltburn Smuggler's Heritage Centre (01287) 625252 is set in ancient fishermen's cottages, and shows period costumed characters with authentic sounds and smells! While you're there, learn all about the 'King of the Smugglers' who was at the centre of the illicit trade 200 years ago. Open Easter to end-Sept 10am - 6pm.

Bunnyland (01287 642228) is situated on the B1366 just off the A171 between Whitby and Guisborough. See the rabbits, guinea pigs and other animals including small pigs and pygmy goats. The animals are kept in beautiful surroundings and you can also walk around a lovely wooded area. Open all year, 10am- 6pm.

Walk 24: Danby to Clitherbeck

Allow: 1 hour 30 minutes

A great walk across the moors with fantastic views over Eskdale. The walk begins from the picturesque village of Danby, which has claimed its place in the history books through its castle. Catherine Parr resided here before she became the sixth wife of Henry VIII. The ruins of this once grand castle have since been incorporated into a farmhouse and are not open to the public.

The walk takes you north towards Danby Low Moor and returns along the valley of Clitherbeck. This valley was once an important coal mining area but was forced out of business by the higher quality coal mined in Durham. Once you have returned to Danby you can get refreshments in the pub or teashop. The Moors Centre is just up the road with lots of information about the area.

Map: Ordnance Survey 1:25000 Explorer OL27 – grid reference 709086

Distance: 2¾ miles (4.4km)

Getting there: Take the road to the Moors Centre from the centre of the village of Danby. Park in the small parking area on the left just up this road or in the lay-by area on the right straight after this.

Walk away from village centre in the direction of the Moors Centre. Turn left up the bridleway straight after a terrace of houses on the left (the last house in the terrace is called Briar Hill House).

The bridleway takes you up to the house and then bends to the right and up the hill. Turn left when the track forks and walk up through the gorse to the moors. The track takes you to two adjacent gateways. Go through the gateway on the right and continue on the track straight ahead.

There are great views behind you over Danby and Eskdale.

Track along Southward Brow

1. Turn right as the track joins another and walk towards the wall. The track then immediately forks again. Take the left-hand fork straight across the moors (Lord's Turnpike) and not the right-hand route along the wall.

   Follow the track all the way to the road. Turn right, cross the bridge and continue up the road for a short distance.

2. Take the next bridleway on the right with a sign for Clitherbeck Farm. Walk straight along this track ignoring the turning down to the farm on the right. Cross over a stream (Clither Beck) and then turn right through a gate (with stile alongside).

   Walk straight ahead through the field keeping the stream to your right. Go through another gateway (marked 'leave gate as found') and walk straight down alongside the stream.

3. Cross the stream then follow the track to the left of a small house and outbuildings.

   Turn right just before the next gate (gatepost has a faint painted

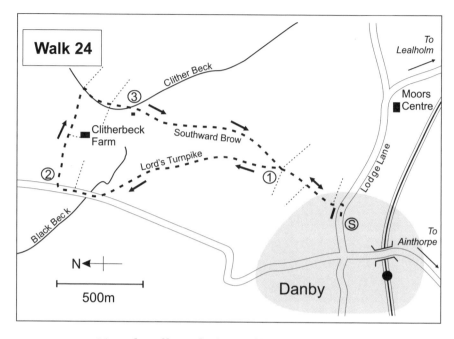

arrow on it) and walk with the wall on your left up to a further gateway. Go through the gate (stile alongside) and make your own way through the bracken, keeping the stone wall in sight to your left.

This section can be hard going at times and the best route to take is seasonally dependent!

Shortly you will see a very obvious farm track that runs alongside the wall. Make your way to this track and follow it until you reach the corner of the wall. Continue straight ahead for a short distance then turn left down the hill when the track forks. Go through the gateway and follow the track down to the road. Turn right and walk down the road until you find your car.

In the area:

Kirkleatham Owl Centre (01642 480512) is home to around 100 birds with hawks, falcons, buzzards and vultures as well as owls from all over the world. Daily flying displays are held and you can meet the baby owls. Open all year, Tuesday to Sunday, 10am – 4.30pm.

Nature's World at Acklam, near Guisborough (www.naturesworld.org.uk), is an ecological centre where you can journey to the future in Futureworld 2020, learn about the flora and fauna of the area and follow the family trails around the centre. For extra fun there are race buggies, go-karts, ride-on tractors and a 400m slide.

Walk 25: Commondale to Danby

Allow: *2 hours 30 minutes (not including train ride)*

→   WC £

This walk follows the Eskdale mainline railway between the villages of Commondale and Danby. The route passes through farmland, beautiful woodland and moorland, and there are spectacular views along the valley to Danby Moors to the north and Commondale Moor to the south. Commondale village is unusual for the area in that it has brick buildings rather than stone. In the 1950s the village had its own brickworks which produced the distinctive red-orange Commondale brick. The village was once called Colmandale, after Colman, Bishop of Lindisfarne, who stopped here on his way to Whitby Abbey.

The route follows very well defined bridleways and minor roads and is easy going apart from a few inclines. Toilets, pubs and tea rooms can be found in Commondale, Castleton (slightly off route) and Danby, which is also home to the Moors Centre – a national park visitor centre with good facilities.

Map: Ordnance Survey 1:25000 Explorer OL26 – grid reference 665100

Distance: 4 miles (6.4km)

Getting there:
By Train: Park a car in Danby village. Take the train two stops to Commondale. From Commondale station, walk up the path to turn right onto the track at Fowl Green Farm.
By car: Leave a car in Danby village. From Danby follow the signs to Castleton. In the centre of Castleton turn right towards Guisborough, cross over the river and head up onto the moors. Turn left into Commondale. Park on the road by the pub. Walk down the road signposted to the station, round a left bend. Turn off the road down the track at Fowl Green Farm
N.B. There is the option of cutting this walk short at Castleton, halfway between the two villages (number 2). You can either leave a car here to do the first half of the walk from Commondale or get the train to do the second half to Danby.

Walk past Fowl Green Farm and continue along the track following the blue bridleway sign to Castleton. Continue straight ahead and through a gate. Go round the bend to the left past a house following the bridleway. Ignore a footpath over a stile. Go through a second gate and continue along the track.

There are views of the Eskdale railway line to your right with Commondale Moor rising bleakly above the opposite side of the valley.

Commondale

1. Pass small patches of birch woodland on either side of the track, which have picnic tables and short easy access routes if you want an extra walk. Go through a third gateway and head down hill (fairly steep) and past a house on your right.

   Walk along the track with the railway down to your right. Pass a second house on your right and simply follow the track until you reach the road.

2. Turn right onto the road, looking out for traffic and head downhill towards Castleton.

   If you want to cut the walk short, the road heads down into Castleton village, with toilets, shops, pubs and a station.

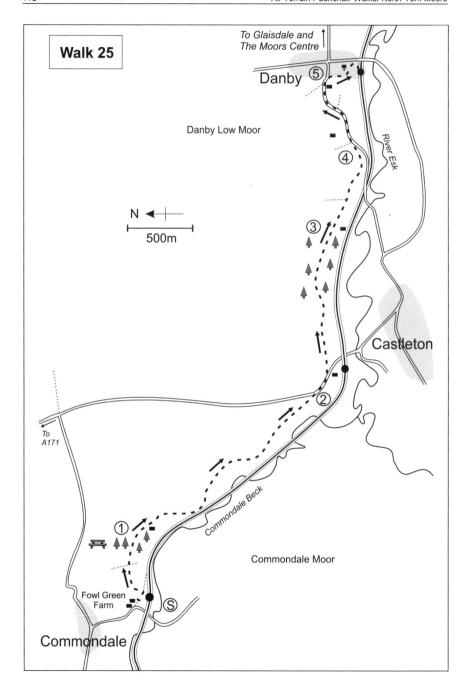

Walk 25

To Glaisdale and
The Moors Centre

Danby ⑤

Danby Low Moor

River Esk

N ◄─┼─
├──────┤
500m

④

③

Castleton

②

To
A171

Commondale Beck

Commondale Moor

①

Fowl Green
Farm   Ⓢ

Commondale

After about 100m, cross the road and join a bridleway signposted to Danby. Head up the track, through a gate and past two lovely houses.

You now get good views across to Castleton to your right. The castle after which the village was named is no longer present but if you look carefully you may see the remains of the motte, the mound on which it stood. The stone from which the castle was built has been "recycled" into the walls of nearby Danby Castle!

Go through a second gate into Danby Park woods. The track gets narrow and rougher here as it heads through pretty birch woodland.

3. Go through a third gate and leave the woods as you head back onto heather moorland. Continue along the track, which is fairly level.

When you reach a junction of footpaths, head along the level track signposted the "Esk Valley Walk". Head downhill towards Danby, with pleasant views of the valley.

4. At the end of the bridleway, turn right down a short stretch of driveway to meet the road. Cross the road and turn left to follow it into Danby. Ignore the first footpath sign on the right (yellow arrow and stile).

5. After about ¼ mile take the second footpath on your right. Continue along the path as it joins a metalled road and walk past houses into the village. Go over a bridge, and turn right to get back to Danby Station.

In the area:

The Moors Centre (01439 772737) is located just outside Danby in the Esk Valley. Originally a shooting lodge for Dawnay Family, the centre is set in 13 acres of grounds and has a pleasant garden, picnic and play area in front of the house and easy walks laid out in the adjacent Crow's Wood. There is a café, toilets and information centre in the house.

Botton Village is run by the Camphill Trust (www.camphill.org.uk) and provides community living and meaningful employment for adults with learning difficulties. Located in the beautiful Danby Dale, the village is open to visitors all year (except Bank Holidays) and you can visit the workshops, gift shops and Coffee Bar (workshops closed Sundays).

Walk 26: Guisborough Forest Trail

Allow: *2 hour 45 minutes*

Guisborough Forest is the largest area of woodland in Cleveland. The forest caters well for visitors with an informative visitor centre, which is the start of our walk. The visitor centre offers various activities such as pond dipping and seasonal events throughout the year. There is a playground in the car park, an adventure playground in the wood and picnic tables by the visitor centre.

The walk is on forest tracks and paths and is good going, but can be muddy in wet weather. There are many routes through the forest but if you decide to go exploring some of the paths do have steps on them and others are used by mountain bikes.

Map: Ordnance Survey 1:25000 Explorer OL26 – grid reference 584152

Distance: 3½ miles (5.6km)

Getting there: Turn off the A173 Guisborough to Stokesley road at the Guisborough Forest Visitor Centre and park in the car park. Free parking, car park closes at 6.30 pm but later parking is available on the exit road. Toilets and baby changing facilities in the visitor centre.

From the car park, walk past the visitor centre and down the broad track marked by a sculpture of a frog.

> This track is the old Middlesborough to Guisborough railway. It was opened in 1853 and used to transport iron ore to the blast furnaces on Teeside. The railway, which later took passengers, finally closed in 1964. Look out for the adventure playground and picnic site in the trees on your right.

Continue along the broad track passing several ponds on your left until you come to a T-junction.

Sculptures in Guisborough Forest

1. At the junction, turn right and through a wide kissing gate marked by sculptures of a kingfisher and newt.

These figures form part of the forest's sculpture trail which features a series of wood carvings done by chainsaw! See how many different animals you can spot on the walk.

Head up the forest track past two sandstone gate-posts and continue uphill towards a house. These tracks can get muddy in wet weather. Follow the path as it bends round to the left and at the next T-junction turn left, away from the house.

2. Continue along this track and at the next junction go straight ahead, ignoring a path zigzagging up into the woods, and then bear right up a gated, broad forest track. Continue up the track into the woods with fields below you on your left.

There are benches on route to pause for a rest and to admire the views, but look out for mountain bikers who come down this hill fast!

3. Ignore a path to your right marked by a yellow arrow and

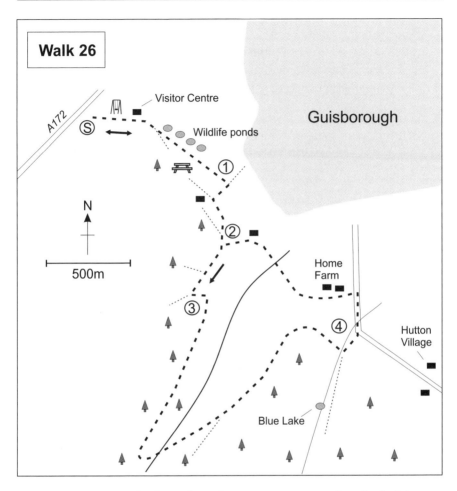

continue along the broad track as it curves round to the left ignoring further paths up to the right. At the next junction of tracks, turn left to follow the edge of the fields below you and continue along this track until you reach a gate.

Go through the gate and follow the path ahead across the fields to a junction with a bridleway. Turn left here and walk down the track.

For a pleasant detour, turn right here and follow the bridleway (an old ironstone railway track) through a gate up to Blue Lake. Built in

1880 by J.W. Pease, the lake was a reservoir to supply water for hydraulic machinery at Home Farm. The lake was given its name because of alum salts washed into it, giving it a blue colour. The lake fell into disuse and has only recently been cleared out.

4. At the end of the track, go through the gate onto a minor road and turn left, watching out for traffic. After about 100m, turn left just past a 30mph sign down a track past Home Farm.

Hutton Village to the right, was originally built to house miners but was rebuilt in the mid 19th century as a model village for the estate workers for Hutton Hall. The Hall was built in 1866, also by JW Pease. The village had a mission house and a school.

Follow this track round to the right to cross open fields. Turn left to walk around the house following the white arrow.

The raised area on the right is a continuation of the old railway.

At the T-junction, turn right and follow the lower track back through the forest. At the next junction, fork right to follow the arrows down a path running downhill into the woods. Continue along this path until you reach the kissing gate you passed through earlier.

Go through the kissing gate and turn left to walk past the ponds back to the visitor centre and your car.

In the area:

Saltburn Cliff Lift (01287 622528) is the oldest remaining cliff lift in Britain dating from 1884. Powered by water balance, the lift links Saltburn pier with the town 120ft up the cliff! Open Easter – September.

Neptune Centre, Ormsby Road, Middlesbrough, has 2 swimming pools, a health and fitness suite and that all important relaxation aid – a crèche!! Phone for details and opening times (01642 230106).

Walk 27: Roseberry Topping

Allow: 2 hours 30 minutes

Roseberry Topping is an iconic landmark in the North York Moors. It stands at just 322m (1,056ft) but, because of its isolation, can be seen from miles around. The hill used to be a cone shape but was mined for alum, ironstone, jet and sandstone. A combination of extensive mining and the presence of a geological fault caused a huge landslip in 1912 leaving the curious profile we see today. The hill has been revered for many years and was worshiped by the Danes who named it 'Othenesburg' or Odin's Hill after the Norse god of creation.

This is not a walk for the faint hearted as there is a lot of uphill pushing to do. The route does not go to the peak but climbs round it and the paths can be very muddy and hard going in winter. However, once the initial climb is completed it is, apart from a couple of stiles, easy going from there on. The views are fantastic so make sure you pick a clear day and take a picnic with you!

Map: Ordnance Survey 1:25000 Explorer OL26 – grid reference 570128

Distance: 3½ miles (5.6km)

Getting there: Park in the Roseberry Topping car park in Newton under Roseberry. There are toilets in the car park.

Walk to the left-hand side of the car park (when facing Roseberry Topping) and turn right onto the bridleway in the direction of the hill. Go through the gateway and continue on the broad track straight ahead.

1. Turn left immediately before the next gateway. Follow the path through a third gateway and continue straight ahead, ignore a gateway on the right. The path now becomes narrow and heads uphill but eventually opens out into heather moorland.

   Turn right when the path forks following the blue arrow, which

Where's Roseberry Topping?

directs you up a steep slope. Turn right at the crossroads towards
the peak of Roseberry Topping.

There are great views over Captain Cook's Monument on Easby
Moor straight ahead. The monument was erected in 1827 and
stands on the summit (1,064ft) of the moor. The monument is said
to overlook Captain Cook's country, and his boyhood home in Great
Ayton lies at the base of the hill.

2. At the next crossroads go through the gateway straight ahead.

If you want to go to the summit of Roseberry Topping take the path
to the right. However, this path is definitely not pushchair friendly.

Continue along this broad path as it gradually heads down hill
through a gateway and to a farm. Turn right immediately before
the farm buildings, through another gateway alongside a cattle
grid (marked with a yellow arrow) and towards a stone house.
The track veers to the left of the house and through a further gateway. Turn right and follow the right-hand edge of the field.

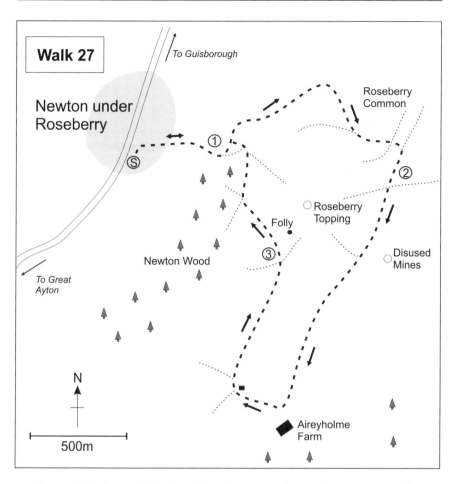

Walk 27

Newton under Roseberry

To Guisborough

Roseberry Common

① ↔

Ⓢ

②

○ Roseberry Topping

Folly

Newton Wood

③

○ Disused Mines

To Great Ayton

N

500m

Aireyholme Farm

Turn right immediately after the trees through a gateway along-side a stile (the gate looks locked but can easily be opened at the hinge end!). Follow the track in the direction of Roseberry Topping.

3. Lift the pushchair over the next stile, and turn left towards the woodland.

   If you want to go and look at the small folly then go up the steep slope and turn left to the folly at the top. To return to the main route go down the slope just to the right of the folly and walk to the gate at the far corner of the field.

Lift the pushchair over the fence before the woodland and turn right onto the track. Follow this track alongside the fence until you pass two gates on the right. The track then goes downhill via a series of shallow stone steps.

Continue straight ahead when you come to a crossroads with a stone marker in the centre. The path heads downhill and veers to the left bringing you to another kissing gate.

Lift the pushchair over the fence next to the kissing gate and follow the track back to your car.

In the area:

Flatt's Lane Woodland Country Park near Guisborough offers superb views and lovely walks around the park. There are exhibitions in the visitor centre and the rangers run family events throughout the year.

Newnham Grange Leisure Farm near Middlesborough (01642 515729) is a unique farm experience where you can see how farming has changed from the 17th century to the present day. Younger visitors can see the animals in the farmyard and byres and can visit the hatchery to see young chicks being born and raised. Demonstrations are arranged through the summer and there is a play area and picnic site. Open April to October all week, weekends all year.

Walk 28: Tidy Brown Hill and Battersby Bank

Allow: 1hour 45minutes

Take a walk along a section of the Cleveland Way as it runs through heather moorland on the top of the Cleveland Hills. These hills domi-nate the scenery in the north-west of this national park. The hill paths that walkers frequent today are those that were laid down in ancient times by drovers, monks and packhorse men. Our route takes you over Battersby Moor and around Tidy Brown Hill with spectacular panoramic views throughout. Tidy does not refer to the state of upkeep of this hill but is a corruption of 'tiddy' which is the local dialect for small! The walk returns via Ingleby Bank, a fantastic viewpoint for the north western reaches of the North York Moors Park.

There is a rocky section on the return route of this circular walk. If you are taking a very young baby you can avoid this section by simply doing a 'there-and-back' walk to Tidy Brown Hill.

Map: Ordnance Survey 1:25000 Explorer OL26 – grid reference 610069

Distance: 3½ miles (5.6km)

Getting there: Travel along the road between Kildale and Easby and take the turning for Baysdale Farm (this is also signposted as the Cleveland Way). Continue along the road for approximately two miles, passing over two cattle grids along the way. Park your car on the side of the road when you come to a sharp left-hand turn with a gateway straight ahead.

Walk past the gate following the blue arrow and Cleveland Way to Bloworth.

Captain Cook's Monument can be seen to your right on the top of Easby Moor (see Walk 27).

Go through the next gate and stay on the path ahead all the way up to

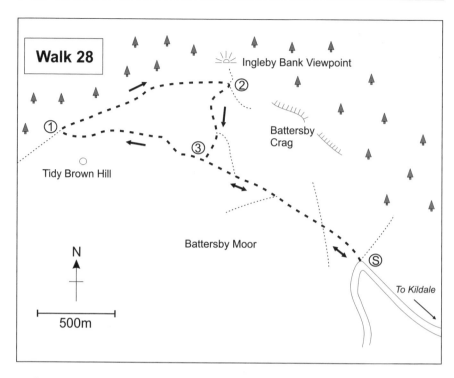

Tidy Brown Hill (a small hill summit). Eventually you will come to a gate at a T-junction.

Ahead are the ridges of Urra and Greenhow Moors and Hasty Bank. Urra Moor is the highest point in the national park (454m).

1. Turn right and follow the track as it heads downhill.

You will now have fantastic views over Captain Cook's Monument and Roseberry Topping straight ahead.

2. At the crossroads where the main path bends to the left turn right up the path with a chain across the entrance (marked with a blue arrow).

You will immediately come to a junction; take the grass path on the right. This path takes you up the hill and across a small stream.

3. At the top of the hill you will come to a T-junction. Turn left, back onto the main track, and follow it all the way back to your car.

In the area:

The Falconry Centre at Kirkby Whiske, near Thirsk, (www.falconrycentre.co.uk) is found at Sion Hill Hall, a lovely stately home, which you can also visit. See birds of prey from around the world and watch them in action during the flying displays. Café and gift shop. Open March – October 10.30-5.30.

Mud, mud, glorious mud!

World of James Herriott is located in the building where the vet lived and worked in Thirsk. You can learn all about being a vet, life in the 1940s and the RTV series 'All Creatures Great and Small'. The centre has a shop and toilets with baby changing facilities and is accessible on all levels. Open all year except Christmas and New Year (www.hambleton.gov.uk/hambleton/herriot.nsf/pages).

Walk 29: Whorlton to Faceby

Allow: *1hour 30minutes*

A pleasant walk between two villages using country lanes and farm tracks. There are great views throughout and a pub at the half-way point! This walk is best undertaken during the summer months as the field paths can be very muddy in winter making pushing hard work.

This walk begins at the ruins of the Church of the Holy Cross, Whorlton. This Norman church is the only remaining structure of the ancient village of Whorlton, which was wiped out by the plague in the 14th century. The church is roofless but the chancel has been preserved and is still in occasional use.

Just down the road from the church is Whorlton Castle. The castle ruins date back to the beginning of the 13th century and overlook the Cleveland Plain. Previous to this there was a Norman motte and bailey castle on this site. Much of the castle was destroyed by Parliamentarians during the Civil War. However, the 14th-century gatehouse tower and tunnel-vaulted cellars still remain. This gatehouse bears the coasts of arms of the Meynells, Darcys and Grays all of whom resided here at some time.

Map: Ordnance Survey 1:25000 Explorer OL26 – grid reference 483025

Distance: 3 miles (4.8km)

Getting there: Take the turning to Swainby from the A172. Drive through the village and turn left immediately before the church (signposted to castle and old church). Park on the roadside next to the old church.

Walk up the road with the old church on your right and the castle behind you. Follow the road as it bends to the right and heads towards some houses (Whorlton).

1. The road ends at a farm (Whorlton House). Turn left through a gateway and into a field; do not go through the gateway straight ahead.

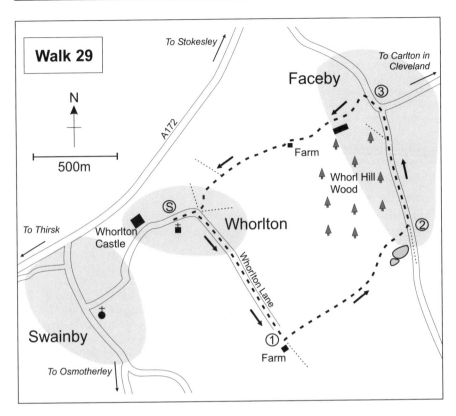

Pass through a second gateway and follow the track along the right-hand edge of the field.

The hill to your left is Whorl Hill. To your right are the ridges of Carlton Moor and Whorlton Moor.

At the top of the field there are two gateways. Go through the left-hand gate and continue along the edge of the field. At the far corner go through the small wooden gate and continue along the path.

At the right-hand corner of the field go through another gateway with a step down and follow the track straight ahead.

2. Go through the next gateway towards the houses ahead. Turn left onto the road and follow it down into the village of Faceby. Turn

left at the junction at the end of the road (Sutton Arms ahead) in the direction of Swainby.

3. Walk down the road a short distance and turn left after you have passed the last house on the right (a white building). Follow the lane up the hill towards Whorl Hill Farm. Go through the farm buildings and turn right just before the farm house (there is a private sign ahead). Then turn left immediately after the house onto a grass path and down through the gateway ahead.

Whorlton church

Follow the track ahead to a further gateway. Stay on the track as it heads downhill to two adjacent gates. Go through the small gate on the left and follow the track on the right-hand edge of the field. Then go through another gateway onto a path between two hedges.

Pass through a further gate and stay on the path ahead. You will be able to see the castle and church in front of you. Go through a final gate and back onto the road. Turn right and find your car next to the church.

In the area:

Stokesley Leisure Centre (01642 711140) offers a variety of sporting activities including two swimming pools. The pools have recently been refurbished and there is a brand new sauna in the pool area.

Captain Cook's Schoolroom Museum (01642 724296) in Great Ayton is set in the charity school where Cook was educated. There is a reconstructed 18th-century schoolroom, where you can see how the great man spent his lessons and how different things were back then! Lift to access first floor. Gift shop. Open April – October

Walk 30: Cod Beck Reservoir, Osmotherley

Allow: 1 hour

An easy walk around a picturesque reservoir that is perfect any time of year but especially good on a hot summer's day. Toddlers will love it as there are picnic tables, grassy banks, woodland to play in and streams to paddle in. Make sure you don't go alone as there are a couple of fences to lift pushchairs over (due to annoyingly narrow kissing gates) and a stream crossing!

The reservoir was completed in 1953 and gets its name from the small river that fills it, Cod Beck, which is a tributary of the River Swale. The name of this beck is derived from the Celtic word 'coed' meaning trees. The reservoir is a breeding ground for the common toad, which is the only species of toad native to this country. Numbers of toads in the UK are declining and many hundreds are killed crossing busy roads especially at spawning time (March-April) when they migrate on mass. Local volunteers man a toad road crossing close to Cod Beck Reservoir during the spawning months. They carry the toads across the roads to ensure get to the reservoir safely.

Map: Ordnance Survey 1:25000 Explorer OL26 – grid reference 468992

Distance: 1½ miles (2.4km)

Getting there: Park in the National Trust car park at the northern end of Cod Beck Reservoir on the road between Osmotherley and Swainby.

Turn left out of the car park and walk a short distance along the road. Take the next path on the left, which leads you down to a kissing gate and the reservoir path.

The car park lies at the beginning of the Lyke Wake Walk a 42 mile route that crosses the North York Moors at its highest and widest points to end on the coast at Ravenscar. The walk was the idea of

Cod Beck Reservoir

a smallholder, Bill Cowley, who in August 1955 challenged walkers to join him in an attempt to reach Ravenscar in just 24 hours!

Lift the pushchair over the fence alongside the kissing gate, as it is too narrow to get through, then follow the woodland path along with the reservoir on your left.

1. Eventually the path will lead you to the far end of the reservoir where there is a picnic table overlooking the dam. Turn left and cross the dam.

2. At the far end of the dam leave the gravel path and turn left across a grass area where there is another picnic table. The grass path soon returns to gravel and follows the edge of the reservoir (on your left) all the way back to the car park.

The path leads you all the way round the reservoir until you eventually come to a few steps and another narrow kissing gate. Lift the pushchair over the fence and turn left down to the stream.

This is a great place for a picnic and for the kids to have a splash around in the water!

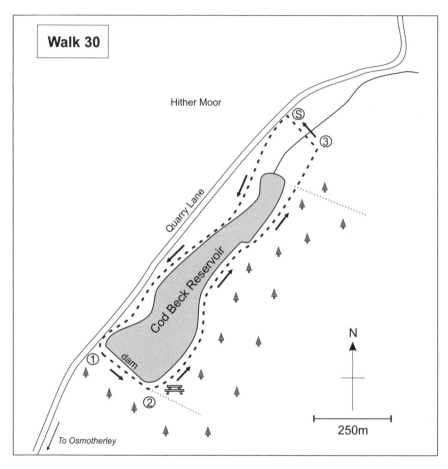

3. Go through the stream (there are a few stepping stones but it is usually shallow enough to wade straight through) and follow the path up the bank on the other side and back to the car park.

In the area:

Mount Grace Priory, (www.englishheritage.org.uk) is found just off the A19 in a tranquil wooded setting below the North York Moors escarpment. The 14th-century ruins show the best preserved Carthusian 'charterhouse' of in Britain. The Carthusian monks lived as hermits, each having a 'two-up, two-down' cell with small garden, where they lived, worked and prayed – 23 of which are clearly defined in the ruins. One of the cells has been rebuilt and furnished to show how it would have looked during monastic occupation. The lovely gardens, which were remodelled in the early 20th century, are home to a wealth of wildlife, including 'Priory Stoats'. Open all year.

Darlington Railway Museum (www.dcrm.org.uk) celebrates the birth of railway! Close to the location of the Stockton to Darlington railway, Britain's first, the museum shows everything from Victorian railway engines to model trains, and you can visit North Road, one of the world's oldest stations. The kids can take part in various activities and you can relax in the Station Café. Family events throughout the year. Open daily 10am-5pm.

More books for intrepid pushchair walkers!

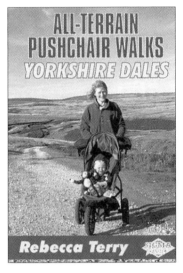

ALL-TERRAIN PUSHCHAIR WALKS: YORKSHIRE DALES

Rebecca Terry

By the same author – 30 pushchair walks in the countryside around the famous dales, including Nidderdale, and near to the major towns of Richmond, Harrogate, Skipton, Settle and Sedbergh. Riverside routes, moorland rambles and strolls around country estates, castles and abbeys. *£7.95*

ALL-TERRAIN PUSHCHAIR WALKS: WEST YORKSHIRE

Rebecca Chippindale & Rebecca Terry

Pushchair-friendly routes in the spectacular countryside around the major towns of Keighley, Bradford, Leeds, Halifax, Huddersfield and Wakefield. Walks visit a wide variety of locations including Ilkley Moor, Hardcastle Crags, Hebden Bridge and the River Wharfe. *£7.95*

ALL-TERRAIN PUSHCHAIR WALKS: SNOWDONIA

Zoë Sayer & Rebecca Terry

30 pushchair-friendly walks through the spectacular scenery of the Snowdonia National Park. The walks range from simple riverside strolls to full-on alpine-style stomps. *£7.95*

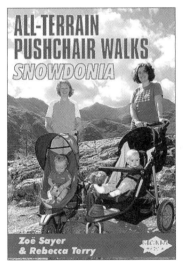

ALL-TERRAIN PUSHCHAIR WALKS: ANGLESEY & LLEYN PENINSULA

Zoë Sayer & Rebecca Terry

Also by Zoë and Rebecca, 30 pushchair-friendly walks in this popular tourist area. Countryside and coastal routes galore! *£7.95*

ALL-TERRAIN PUSHCHAIR WALKS: PEAK DISTRICT

Alison Southern

Level routes around Peak District villages and more adventurous (but safe) hikes across the moors. Alison is a parent of a young child and has an excellent knowledge of the Peak District. So now there's no reason to stay at home – here is the ideal opportunity to introduce the youngest children to the wide-open spaces of the Peak District! *£7.95*

ALL-TERRAIN PUSHCHAIR WALKS: NORTH LAKELAND

Ruth & Richard Irons

30 walks across North Lakeland from Ennerdale Water to Lowther Park, Haweswater to Bassenthwaite. Something to suit every type of walker – from Sunday Strollers to Peak Baggers and everyone else in between! Ruth and Richard Irons are experienced parents and qualified outdoor pursuits instructors – a reliable combination! *£6.95*

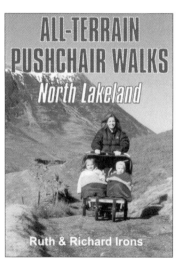

ALL-TERRAIN PUSHCHAIR WALKS: SOUTH LAKELAND

Norman Buckley

"This book is fantastic – a perfect guide for parents" — *Kathleen Jones (Lakeland Book of The Year Awards, 2005).* The companion to our 'All-Terrain Pushchair Walks for North Lakeland' – walks north to south, from Grasmere to Grizedale Forest, and west to east, from Coniston to Kendal – you'll be spoilt for choice! *£6.95*

All of our books are all available through booksellers. For a free catalogue, please contact: **SIGMA LEISURE, 5 ALTON ROAD, WILMSLOW, CHESHIRE SK9 5DY**

Tel/Fax: 01625-531035

E-mail: info@sigmapress.co.uk   Web site: www.sigmapress.co.uk